naturally
balanced
C O O K I N G

About the author

Peter Vaughan is a graduate of the Academy of Culinary Arts. He has worked in top restaurants in the UK, France and the Caribbean, and has received many awards, including the prestigious Annual Award of Excellence.

As a teenager with a weight problem, he turned his attentions to learning about the properties of ingredients and how they fuel the body, and subsequently solved his problems by eating a more natural and balanced diet. His particular interest in health and fitness has led him to study for and obtain specific qualifications in both nutrition and herbalism.

Peter's many appearances on television and radio focus on enjoying the most delicious foods that create the perfect balance for health and fitness. He owns and runs The Healthy Life, a natural food shop, café and dining room in the market town of Devizes, Wiltshire, whose products reflect not only his love of good food but also his culinary expertise and knowledge of the dietary requirements of the twenty-first century.

naturally
balanced
COOKING

peter vaughan

foulsham
LONDON • NEW YORK • TORONTO • SYDNEY

foulsham

The Publishing House, Bennetts Close, Cippenham,
Slough, Berkshire, SL1 5AP, England

ISBN 0-572-02826-1

Printed in Great Britain by St Edmundsbury Press, Bury St Edmunds, Suffolk

Contents

Foreword

I collect cookery books like some people collect stamps, and this one is a real gem – packed full of practical ideas, inspirational menus and fabulously tasty recipes guaranteed to go down well with all the family.

Peter and I first worked together on Carlton TV's *The A-Z of Food & Beauty,* where I appreciated (and sampled!) at first hand his flair for healthily creative cooking. He has a wonderful knack of making superbly tasty food from good-for-you ingredients, effortlessly proving the point that the healthy option can also be the most delicious.

His enthusiasm and dedication to helping everyone make the most of mealtimes has resulted in a very easy-to-follow, foodie treat for us all. Packed with new and original recipes – from quick and simple suppers to plans for more adventurous gourmet menus – there's something here for everyone.

Eating well results in looking and feeling well too – and there's never been a better way to help us achieve this.

Bon appétit!

Liz Earle

Introduction

Why do people find food so fascinating? I believe it is a much deeper issue than just the delicious sensations of taste and smell. Food has the ability to cure not only the body but also the mind, and to bring a feeling of wholeness into people's lives.

Food has always been of significance in my family. My grandparents, mother, brother and I all love cooking and food. As far back as I can remember, there was an emphasis on its importance and its benefits. Fresh was always seen as best. If there was ever a crisis or someone was feeling a bit down, my grandma would bring out the trolley full of home-made goodies, all prepared with love by herself and my grandpa. The world never seemed such a harsh place after the arrival of the groaning tea trolley!

I started my culinary training in a local pub/restaurant. Once I had set my mind on being a chef, my mother insisted that I saw the reality of life in the catering industry, rather than dwelling solely on the creative side of the job. The unsociable hours, hot conditions and immense pressure during service time turned out to be great fun for me and, even though I arrived home exhausted, I loved every minute of it.

My apprenticeship was on a scheme that is now regarded as one of the best chef-training programmes in the UK. Backed by the Academy of Culinary Arts and currently sponsored by Waitrose, such was the rigour and discipline of the course that I now refer to it as the culinary equivalent of the SAS!

During the four years of training, my time was divided between Bournemouth and Poole College and the Intercontinental in Park Lane under the expert eye of Peter Kromberg. He, in particular, encouraged me to be open-minded about food and to use the knowledge and techniques I was being taught to investigate my own style of cuisine. During those four years I met some of the top culinary masters and fed some of the most influential people in Britain. The meals I prepared contained the finest ingredients and each one cost far more than I could earn in a week!

Whilst I enjoyed the work, I really wanted to share the skills I had acquired with a wider audience than could afford this fine dining. Having lost a lot of weight just before starting my training through taking more interest in the properties of ingredients, I also realised that many aspects of this culinary style were working against the body, inhibiting its ability to obtain maximum nutrition from these meals. As a result, I embarked on a gradual change of style, which has culminated in my current interest in body-friendly food. Over the past four years I have worked in television and radio with some of the key figures in the world of health and nutrition.

The food scares of recent years have made many people start to think more carefully about what they are eating. This public awareness has lifted a curtain on how food is produced and what happens to it on its journey from its source to our tables. Some of that information has shocked us and made us realise that we have to pay more attention to what we consume and to choose it more carefully.

This book is for those who want to enjoy and benefit from the food that they eat.

Food for a healthy life

There is a major paradox in the attitude of the Western world to food and health. While interest in food, TV chefs and cookery books continues to grow, the diet of most people in the West remains nutritionally flawed and contributes to many recurring health problems. We have more time and energy to spend on health and leisure pursuits, yet we don't pay enough attention to one of the most fundamental ways of staying healthy: our food. My focus – and what I feel should be the focus for all of us in the twenty-first century – is on how to get healthy and stay healthy, and the basis of that is eating a wholesome, nutritionally sound, healthy diet.

So what is a healthy diet? Sadly, the very words often conjure up images of brown, exceptionally chewy and uninteresting food, and irritating, bouncy people who bore us with their almost evangelical enthusiasm for it. That's not designed to encourage anyone to think more about what they eat. But most of us would like to have more energy and fewer aches and pains and be less prone to infections, and this is exactly what will happen if our bodies are given the correct fuel.

The best way to describe health is to say that it is a state of natural balance, which the body maintains by using the food it is supplied with. A healthy diet is therefore a diet that provides the body with these ingredients it can recognise and accept easily, so that it can digest and utilise the goodness in them. This book is designed to show you that, far from being brown and boring, healthy food can be colourful, exciting, easy to prepare and a pleasure to eat.

Here are some simple guidelines towards providing the best for your body.

Buy fresh

Few people nowadays have time to shop every day for fresh food, but you should try to buy and use food that is as fresh as possible. There may well be a local 'box scheme' for fresh vegetables and fruit that are delivered either to your door or a local collection point, or perhaps you could drop in at your local corner shop on the way home from work if they stock fresh goods. Remember that anything that has an abnormally long shelf life must contain additives that extend its natural life, so be cautious.

Make sure you also include in your diet some of the wide range of grains that are available. They are nutritious and inexpensive and give variety to your meals. We also need to eat lots of nuts and seeds and these are often neglected, partly because some so-called healthy recipes contain too many and are a bit like eating bird seed! When I cook, I combine them with other ingredients and include just enough to give the flavour, texture and goodness.

Use unrefined ingredients

When it comes to foods such as flour and rice, most people think that 'white' looks, tastes and cooks better, and that 'brown' is coarse and chewy, but this thinking is at least a hundred years out of date. Sadly, the polishing, bleaching and other processes that go into refined foods often strip them of a large proportion of their original nutrients. In addition to that, chemicals and additives of all kinds are frequently added to improve their shelf life, colour or flavour. It's clear then that refined foods are not natural ingredients and the body may not recognise them or even like them very much. Try to avoid highly refined foods and go for those that are as near to their natural state as possible.

Eat more fruit and vegetables

There is some evidence that a vegetarian diet may be more likely to maintain good health, although this could be partly because those who choose to be vegetarian are more likely to think about what they are eating and consciously follow a more balanced diet. It is certainly true that you don't have to be vegetarian to be healthy – our bodies are designed to eat meat and fish and both are very nutritious. The problem is that we weren't designed to eat as much meat as we currently consume in the West. According to nutritionists, the perfect balance is 30 per cent meat and fish to 70 per cent fruit, vegetables and grains, and so I have reflected this in my choice of recipes in this book.

As well as being good for us, cutting down on meat and fish is also good for animal welfare. If everyone cut back, we could support our consumption without resorting to farming methods that are often inhumane and, we are beginning to realise, put us at risk as well as the animals. Remember, it takes 10 kg/22 lb of grain to produce 1 kg/2.2 lb of meat – that's a lot of resources going into one meal.

From a health point of view, it is a good idea to try to cut down on the amount of meat you eat, especially red meat, so start by replacing one meat meal a week with a vegetarian option, then begin to move the balance of your diet towards the ideal.

Choose organic and free-range

The debate on organic food – price versus nutritional value – goes on. However, it is clear that if chemicals are being used extensively on food items, a certain residue will be passed on into our bodies and no one really knows the cumulative effect this will have in the long term. Even foods that you thought were really healthy, such as dried fruit, may have been sprayed with oil and most citrus fruit have a coating of wax. Do look out for labels that indicate that the food is in its natural state – unwaxed lemons and unsulphured apricots, for example, are now fairly commonplace. As a general rule, my advice would be to go for organic where your budget will allow but never cut down on the amount of fresh fruit, vegetables and other good ingredients because you are afraid to buy non-organic.

I always buy free-range poultry and eggs. Poultry that have been raised by this method are fed a far more natural diet than their battery-raised counterparts and their meat and eggs have more flavour and a better colour and texture.

Cut down on salt and sugar

Many processed foods and popular drinks contain amazing amounts of salt and sugar. The more you have, the more you want, and both these substances can cause problems if taken in excessive quantities. However, as a chef with a passion for cooking with flavour, texture and nutrition, I could not possibly consider cutting them out completely. Both of them are important to our taste buds and help to draw out flavour – that is why they are used so extensively in the food industry. The message here, as with so many issues relating to food and health, is to strike a balance. Certainly you should never need to add salt to food at the table; it should be perfectly seasoned before it gets there. You can also use herbs, spices and other ingredients that add flavour, thus minimising the need for salt. When I do use salt, I choose sea salt, which is less refined than table salt. As for sugar, there are many other natural sweeteners, so try these out – you will find they give a variety of exciting tastes. If you need to use sugar, choose unrefined caster (superfine) sugar; it has a beige tinge to it but is tastier and more nutritious than the white version.

Look out for fats and oils

This is another area where balance is crucial. Many people in the West are still eating too much fat, particularly saturated fat. But with the advent of low-fat and no-fat diets to help weight loss, the elimination of such items from our diet has in some cases gone to the other extreme, meaning that some people are actually eating too little fat. The fact is, we do need some fat in our diet; the important thing is to make sure we don't have too much, and that it is of the right kind. Essential fatty acids – which really are essential! – cannot be manufactured by the body; they have to be obtained from food. The best way to obtain them is to eat oily fish, nuts and seeds and to use any of the delicious oils made from nuts and seeds. Try to use cold-pressed oils, unrefined if possible, as these are closest to the natural state.

I also recommend avoiding margarine and butter substitutes that contain hydrogenated fats or trans fatty acids. It is believed that our bodies don't recognise these chemically altered fats, which are used to extend the shelf life of the product. Hydrogenated fats have been linked to high blood pressure and heart disease for some time, so are best avoided.

Love your food

The guidelines I have given form the foundation of the recipes I have created for this book, but there are two other crucial elements: great taste and maximum enjoyment. I have tried to offer you as much variety and flexibility as possible, so you will really enjoy cooking and eating the dishes. The fact that they are also doing you good is an added bonus!

The recipes have been designed to fit into various categories: food to enjoy with the family, food for entertaining friends, comfort food, food for when we are out to impress and so on. But you can mix and match the recipes and serve them wherever and whenever you like.

I have absolutely no doubt that food has an uplifting effect on both body and mind. A meal prepared with love will have a profound outcome for both the cook and the people who share it. It may be easy to forget this in the busy rush of our everyday lives when the pressures of the world are on our shoulders, but I do hope that my recipes will bring you enjoyment – not only in the eating but in the cooking as well.

Notes on the recipes

- Do not mix metric, imperial and American measures. Follow one set only. American terms are given in brackets.

- All spoon measurements are level:
  1 tsp = 5 ml; 1 tbsp = 15 ml.

- Eggs are large unless otherwise stated. If you use a different size, adjust the amount of liquid added to obtain the right consistency.

- Fresh produce should be washed, peeled, cored and seeded, where necessary.

- Seasoning and the use of strongly flavoured ingredients, such as onions and garlic, are very much a matter of personal preference. Taste the food and adjust the seasoning as you cook.

- Always use fresh herbs unless dried are specifically called for. If it is necessary to use dried herbs, use half the quantity stated. Chopped frozen varieties are much better than dried but neither can be used for garnishing.

- Can and packet sizes are approximate and will depend on the particular brand.

- Some recipes call for margarine as an alternative to butter. You can use your favourite brand, but since not all margarines are suitable for cooking, check the packet before using for the first time.

- Use your own discretion in substituting ingredients and personalising the recipes. Make notes of particular successes as you go along.

- Use whichever kitchen gadgets you like to speed up preparation and cooking times: mixers for whisking, food processors for grating, slicing, mixing or kneading, liquidisers for liquidising.

- All ovens vary, so cooking times have to be approximate. Adjust cooking times and temperatures according to manufacturer's instructions. Always preheat a conventional oven and cook on the centre shelf unless otherwise specified. Fan ovens do not require preheating.

- Most of the recipes make four portions but you can adjust the recipes for small or larger quantities, or serve two and save two for the following day.

food for VITALITY

The human mind and body are exceedingly complex and we are affected not only by what we eat, but also by how we feel when we eat. Feed your body with top-quality fuel and the rewards are high: you'll enjoy improved stamina, restful sleep and higher energy levels. The recipes in this section include some exceptionally quick-to-prepare dishes because, with all that energy, you will be wanting to get into action! There are also some great high-energy dishes for packed lunches, as it can be difficult to buy energy-boosting food when you are out and about.

Cracked wheat salad with cumin and sunflower seeds

Cracked wheat, also known as bulgar, is simply cracked wheat berries that have been steamed and hulled. Bulgar is an extremely effective food if eaten an hour before exercise as it is a releases its energy slowly. It will help lift your energy levels and sustain them for hours, so it makes a great lunchtime dish.

MAKES 2–3 PORTIONS

100 g/4 oz/1 cup bulgar (cracked wheat)

5 ml/1 tsp ground cumin

2.5 ml/½ tsp ground turmeric

300 ml/½ pt/1¼ cups hot vegetable stock

2 carrots

1 red (bell) pepper

1 yellow pepper

1 green pepper

4 spring onions (scallions)

125 g/4½ oz/generous 1 cup sunflower seeds

Juice of ½ lemon

30 ml/2 tbsp cold-pressed virgin olive oil

Sea salt and freshly ground black pepper

1 Place the bulgar, cumin and turmeric in a medium saucepan or sauté pan and place over a high heat, stirring occasionally, for about 2 minutes until the spices are warm and fragrant.

2 Add the hot stock, bring to the boil, then reduce the heat, cover with a tight-fitting lid and simmer gently for 7–8 minutes until the bulgar has absorbed all the stock.

3 Meanwhile, grate the carrots, evenly dice the peppers and slice the spring onions.

4 Remove the bulgar from the heat and stir in the prepared vegetables. Reserve a few sunflower seeds for garnish and add the remainder with the lemon juice and olive oil. Season to taste with salt and pepper and mix well.

5 Transfer to a serving bowl and sprinkle with the remaining sunflower seeds.

Serving suggestions This is perfect served on its own for lunch, or you could serve it as a side dish to accompany a main course such as Mushroom Fricassee on Toast with Cranberry (see page 67).

Hints and variations If you would like to serve the bulgar as a traditional tabbouleh, then simply leave out the sunflower seeds and add a large bunch of chopped fresh parsley, a little more lemon juice and plenty of cold-pressed virgin olive oil.

NATURALLY BALANCED Bulgar is an excellent source of iron, which is essential for the production of haemoglobin, the oxygen-carrying component in the blood. People who are tired for no apparent reason may be deficient in iron, as this will starve the body of oxygen.

Morning banana porridge with almond and maple syrup

No one should go without breakfast – it sets you up for the day. If you're a newcomer to this idea, then try making this banana porridge during the autumn and winter months. The bananas mash down into the oats and make a delicious porridge, which you can top with almonds and maple syrup.

MAKES 2 PORTIONS

75 g/3 oz/¾ cup rolled porridge oats

120 ml/4 fl oz/½ cup semi-skimmed or soya milk

120 ml/4 fl oz/½ cup water

A pinch of sea salt

2 bananas, peeled and chopped

15 ml/1 tbsp sultanas (golden raisins) or other dried fruit, chopped

15 ml/1 tbsp sunflower seeds

15 ml/1 tbsp pumpkin seeds

15 ml/1 tbsp ground almonds

10 ml/2 tsp maple syrup (optional)

1 Mix together the oats, milk, water, salt and chopped bananas.

2 Cook in the microwave on Full Power, or over a medium heat, for 3–4 minutes until the porridge begins to bubble, then stir again and cook for a further 1 minute until thick.

3 Stir in the sultanas and seeds.

4 Spoon into serving bowls, then sprinkle with the ground almonds and drizzle with maple syrup, if liked.

Serving suggestions Because porridge is such a simple dish, it's also very versatile – you can serve it with whatever you wish. Try it with mixed forest berries spiked with lime juice, or just sprinkle it with some grated apple and crushed nuts, such as walnuts, or for a change, use crushed pistachios and drizzle with clear honey.

NATURALLY BALANCED As porridge or muesli, oats are the perfect morning food to set you up for a day of craziness at work as they are a rich source of vitamin B1. This essential vitamin is required by every cell in the body to process carbohydrates, fat and protein for energy. Nerve cells also need this B-vitamin in order to function effectively.

FOOD FOR VITALITY

Warm lentil and lemon salad with watercress and feta

Puy lentils have a delicious flavour, don't need pre-soaking, and are extremely reasonable in price! Fresh home-made stock is best but you can buy good-quality chilled stock or just use a stock cube. If you are seriously short of time, simply warm some canned lentils.

MAKES 4 PORTIONS

225 g/8 oz/1 cup puy lentils

1 litre/1¾ pts/4¼ cups vegetable stock

1 onion, finely chopped

1 bay leaf

2 bunches of fresh watercress

30 ml/2 tbsp cold-pressed virgin olive oil

15 ml/1 tbsp chopped fresh mint or parsley

Juice of 1 lemon

100 g/4 oz/1 cup feta cheese, finely crumbled

Sea salt and freshly ground black pepper

1 Put the lentils, stock, onion and bay leaf in a large saucepan and bring to the boil. Reduce the heat and leave to simmer for about 20 minutes until the lentils are soft and tender.

2 While the lentils are cooking, cut each bunch of watercress in half, including the stems. Wash and drain, then place in a mixing bowl with the olive oil, chopped herbs and half the lemon juice. Toss in the feta cheese and season with plenty of freshly ground black pepper.

3 When the lentils are ready, strain through a sieve, reserving the liquid for a soup or casserole if you wish (you can freeze it).

4 Add the remaining lemon juice to the lentils and season to taste with salt and pepper.

5 Pile the lentils on to warm plates, then gently pile the feta and watercress salad on top and serve.

Serving suggestions There's no need for accompaniments – this makes a complete lunch dish in itself.

Hints and variations You can use other types of cheese for this dish and also add a little ham or bacon to the lentils as they are cooking. Any leftover lentils and watercress can be mixed together and packed in a lunch box for work the next day.

NATURALLY BALANCED Lentils are packed full of many essential nutrients, as well as being high in fibre. Eating them regularly may help reduce the risk of coronary heart disease, probably because fibre lowers cholesterol levels. Lentils are also extremely rich in the mineral potassium, which plays a critical role in the transmission of electrical impulses in the heart.

Roasted spiced couscous with chickpea and spinach salad

Many people find that couscous becomes starchy and heavy when they prepare it. You will not have such problems with this recipe, as the couscous is lightly roasted before you add the liquid. This imparts more flavour and texture and also prevents the granules from sticking together.

MAKES 4 PORTIONS

200 g/7 oz/generous 1 cup couscous

2.5 ml/½ tsp ground cumin

2.5 ml/½ tsp ground coriander (cilantro)

2.5 ml/½ tsp ground turmeric

A pinch of cayenne

400 ml/14 fl oz/1¾ cups hot vegetable stock

FOR THE SALAD

1 x 425 g/15 oz/large can of chickpeas (garbanzos), drained

1 carrot, grated

A handful of baby spinach leaves

2 tomatoes, cut into small dice

50 g/2 oz/⅓ cup sultanas (golden raisins)

1 red (bell) pepper, seeded and chopped

1 green pepper, seeded and chopped

1 x 200 g/7 oz/small can of sweetcorn (corn), drained

Juice of ½ lemon

1 Sprinkle the couscous and spices into a large dry frying pan (skillet) and heat gently for about 5 minutes, shaking the pan occasionally, until the granules have turned a deep golden colour.

2 Stir in the hot vegetable stock and remove the pan from the heat. Cover with a tight-fitting lid and leave to stand for 10 minutes until the couscous has absorbed all the stock and is nice and fluffy.

3 Toss all the salad ingredients together lightly.

4 Stir the couscous into the salad, then transfer to a serving dish.

Serving suggestions This dish makes a delicious lunch dish on its own, or you can serve it as an accompaniment to Moroccan Chickpea and Coriander Casserole (see page 74).

Hints and variations Both the spiced couscous and the salad work well separately. The couscous also makes a great lunch box for the kids to take to school or for you to take to work. You can make it at the beginning of the week and it will last for three days in the fridge – or longer in the freezer. Then you can just add your favourite ingredients each day.

NATURALLY BALANCED Combining cereals and pulses in the same meal provides the body with complete protein, needed to maintain the continuous growth and repair of the human body. Like bulgar, couscous is a slow-energy-release food, which means that it raises your blood sugar level at a gradual rate, so that energy levels are maintained at a more constant rate throughout the day.

FOOD FOR VITALITY

Butter bean and bacon salad

You can cook your own dried butter (lima) beans if you prefer, but I think it's much easier to use canned beans – they are just as nutritious and save lots of time, making this a great last-minute dish. You can leave out the bacon if you prefer, although it does help enhance the creamy taste and texture of the butter beans.

MAKES 2 LARGE PORTIONS

200 g/7 oz good-quality back bacon, rinded and chopped

1 onion, finely chopped

200 g/7 oz ripe cherry tomatoes, halved

30 ml/2 tbsp chopped fresh parsley

15 ml/1 tbsp white wine vinegar

10 ml/2 tsp clear honey

5 ml/1 tsp Dijon mustard

5 ml/1 tsp wholegrain mustard

45 ml/3 tbsp sunflower oil

1 x 225 g/8 oz/small can of butter beans, drained

Sea salt and freshly ground black pepper

1 Heat a non-stick frying pan (skillet) without any oil, then add the bacon and dry-fry for 2–3 minutes.

2 Add the onion and cherry tomatoes and continue to cook for a further 2 minutes.

3 Meanwhile, reserve a pinch of the parsley for garnish and mix the remainder in a bowl with the vinegar, honey and mustards. Keep whisking the mixture and slowly add the oil a drop at a time until the mixture thickens and emulsifies.

4 Stir the butter beans into the bacon, then spoon the mixture into the dressing, add seasoning to taste and mix everything together well.

5 Spoon into warm bowls and sprinkle with the reserved parsley before serving.

Serving suggestions This dish is delicious served with mixed salad leaves and warm bread for lunch. Alternately, you could serve it as part of buffet with a variety of salads.

*Hints and variation*s Try experimenting with other types of bean, such as haricot (navy) or red kidney beans. Each has its own unique flavour and they all work well with bacon.

NATURALLY BALANCED Always try to source the best bacon you can; I like to use organic bacon if at all possible. Cheaper commercial bacon has often had a large percentage of nitrates and water pumped into it. This can be seen as a white substance that rises to the surface of the bacon as it cooks.

Baked potatoes with a twist

Nothing can really beat a good baked potato for lunch or supper, but if you and your family are running out of inspiring ways to serve them, just try this. It couldn't be simpler to prepare – and my TV audience loved it!
See photograph opposite page 48.

MAKES 2 PORTIONS

2 medium to large baking potatoes

2 tomatoes, sliced

100 g/4 oz Mozzarella cheese, sliced

1 ripe avocado, peeled, stoned (pitted) and sliced

Sea salt and freshly ground black pepper

30 ml/2 tbsp cold-pressed virgin olive oil

1 Preheat the oven to 200°C/400°F/gas 6/fan oven 180°C or the grill (broiler) to maximum.

2 Wash and wipe the potatoes and prick all over with a fork. Cook them in the microwave on Full Power for 10–12 minutes or until just cooked.

3 Using a serrated knife, make five deep incisions across the top of each cooked potato, leaving the skin underneath completely joined.

4 Place the potatoes in a baking dish. Insert the tomatoes, Mozzarella and avocado slices into the incisions in the potatoes, sprinkle with a little salt and pepper and drizzle with the olive oil.

5 Bake in the preheated oven for 10 minutes or cook under the grill until the cheese has melted and turned lightly golden brown.

6 Serve with any oil or cooking juices poured over the top.

Serving suggestions These make a great lunch on their own, or you can serve them as a main meal with a crisp, fresh salad.

Hints and variations You can prepare the dish well in advance: precook the potatoes and layer them with the avocado, cheese and tomatoes (brush the avocado with a little lemon juice to prevent it from browning). Then place in the preheated oven for 15 minutes just before you are ready to serve. You can also try other filling combinations, such as courgettes (zucchini) with goats' cheese or bacon and tomato.

NATURALLY BALANCED Many of the nutrients in a potato are found a few millimetres below the skin. These are lost once the potatoes are peeled and cooked, so it is best to cook and eat them with their skins on.

Salmon and horseradish on toasted bagels

This recipe makes use of canned salmon, which is a great storecupboard standby. It is best to use every bit of the contents of the can, as the bones become soft, because of the high cooking temperature used in the canning process, and can be mashed into the salmon spread.

MAKES 4 SNACK PORTIONS OR 2 LUNCH PORTIONS

2 bagels

1 x 185 g/6 oz/small can of wild or red salmon, drained

4 spring onions (scallions), chopped

15 ml/1 tbsp tomato ketchup (catsup)

15 ml/1 tbsp crème fraîche

10 ml/2 tsp creamed horseradish

Juice of 1 lemon

1 bunch of fresh coriander (cilantro) leaves, chopped

A few drops of Tabasco sauce or a pinch of cayenne

Sea salt and freshly ground black pepper

15 ml/1 tbsp cold-pressed virgin olive oil

1 bunch of fresh watercress

10 ml/2 tsp sesame seeds

1 Cut the bagels in half and toast until golden brown. Stack upright to help keep them crisp while they rest.

2 Meanwhile, place the salmon and spring onions in a large mixing bowl. Add the ketchup, crème fraîche, horseradish, half the lemon juice, the chopped coriander and Tabasco sauce or cayenne. Use a fork to mix all the ingredients together well, and season to taste with pepper. It does not really need salt, but add a little if you wish.

3 In another bowl, whisk together the oil and the remaining lemon juice and season with salt and pepper, then gently toss with the watercress.

4 Spread the salmon mixture over the toasted bagels, then sprinkle with sesame seeds.

5 Serve the bagels with the watercress salad on the side.

Hints and variations If you want to prepare these in advance for a picnic or lunch box, spread the bagels with a little butter or unhydrogenated margarine before spreading them with the salmon pâté as this will help stop the bagel becoming soggy.

NATURALLY BALANCED Calcium, which is found in the fish bones, is an important mineral. It helps build and repair bone structure and also aids in the maintenance of the brain and nervous system. You can obtain ample amounts of calcium from green vegetables, herbs, milk and poppy seeds.

Oriental coleslaw

I picked up this delicious recipe on my travels and it's so delicious, I now use it all the time. It's crisp and refreshing but, unlike most coleslaws, this oriental version does not use mayonnaise.

MAKES 6–8 PORTIONS

45 ml/3 tbsp toasted sesame oil

30 ml/2 tbsp soy sauce

15 ml/1 tbsp clear honey

15 ml/1 tbsp white wine vinegar

Juice of 1 lime

1 small red cabbage, quartered, cored and thinly sliced

4 carrots, grated

1 bunch of spring onions (scallions), thinly sliced

1 garlic clove, finely crushed

1 bunch of fresh coriander (cilantro) leaves, chopped

1 Whisk together the sesame oil, soy sauce, honey, vinegar and lime juice.

2 Mix together the cabbage, carrot, spring onions, garlic and half the coriander.

3 Pour the dressing over and toss everything together well, then leave for 5–10 minutes to allow the flavours to develop.

4 Transfer to a serving bowl and sprinkle with the remaining coriander.

Serving suggestions As a side dish, this goes well with grilled (broiled) meats and rich main courses.

NATURALLY BALANCED Sinigrin, a plant chemical recently identified in cabbage, is thought to help deactivate some cancerous cells in the bloodstream.

Caribbean coleslaw

This coleslaw starts off with the traditional ingredients of cabbage, carrot and fennel – but there the similarity ends. The hot, tangy dressing gives it a truly tropical flavour, guaranteed to liven up everyone's taste buds.

MAKES 6–8 PORTIONS

100 ml/3½ fl oz/scant ½ cup mayonnaise

1 red chilli, seeded and finely chopped

Juice of 1 lime

15 ml/1 tbsp unrefined caster (superfine) sugar

15 ml/1 tbsp Worcestershire sauce

A few drops of Tabasco sauce or a pinch of cayenne

Sea salt, to taste

1 small white cabbage, quartered, cored and finely shredded

4 carrots, finely grated

1 fennel bulb, coarsely grated

1 bunch of spring onions (scallions), chopped

1 bunch of fresh chives, finely snipped

1 Whisk together the mayonnaise, chilli, lime juice, sugar, Worcestershire sauce and Tabasco sauce or cayenne. Season to taste with salt and a little more sugar, if liked.

2 Mix together the cabbage, carrots, fennel and spring onions. Reserve a few chives for garnish, then mix in the remainder.

3 Pour the dressing over the salad stuffs and toss together well.

4 Transfer to a serving bowl.

Serving suggestions This wonderful medley of flavours goes well with cold meats. You could also try serving it with my Baked Potato with a Twist (see page 20).

NATURALLY BALANCED Cabbage juice is a popular health drink in Northern Europe, but as it unfortunately tends to produce a lot of wind, I would recommend sticking to my coleslaw.

Smoked mackerel and mango salad with avocado

I first came up with this combination when I appeared on a chat show on BBC1. The presenter, Vanessa Feltz, said that it sounded disgusting, but a member of the audience who tasted it, claimed that it tasted sensational! I certainly think it's a great way to liven up smoked mackerel.

MAKES 4 PORTIONS

4 fillets of smoked mackerel, peppered or plain

150 g/5 oz/1¼ cups pumpkin seeds

1 ripe mango, peeled, stoned (pitted) and thinly sliced

1 ripe avocado, peeled, stoned and thinly sliced

Juice of 1 lemon

30 ml/2 tbsp cold-pressed virgin olive oil

5 ml/1 tsp creamed horseradish

5 ml/1 tsp Dijon mustard

400 g/14 oz mixed salad leaves

5 ml/1 tsp clear honey

1 Preheat the grill (broiler) to high, then place the mackerel fillets on a tray under the grill for 3–4 minutes until warm.

2 Meanwhile, place the pumpkin seeds in a small frying pan (skillet) and heat rapidly for about 3 minutes until lightly coloured, shaking the pan occasionally.

3 Remove the skin from the back of the fish, then break up the mackerel flesh into small pieces with a fork. Mix the flaked mackerel with the mango and avocado.

4 Whisk the lemon juice, olive oil, horseradish and mustard in a bowl until well blended.

5 Add the salad leaves, mackerel, mango and avocado to the dressing and toss gently.

6 Stir the honey into the pumpkin seeds.

7 Spoon the salad on to individual plates or bowls and sprinkle with the sweetened pumpkin seeds to serve.

Hints and variations You can use any type of smoked fish for this salad, so if you are not fond of mackerel you can try it with smoked trout. You can also experiment with toasting other types of seeds, such as sunflower and sesame.

NATURALLY BALANCED Mackerel is one of the cheapest and most readily available fish. It is extremely rich in the essential omega-3 fatty acids and also in the mineral selenium, which may reduce the risk of cancer.

Spinach mimosa salad with toasted sunflower seeds

This quick energy-boosting salad makes an ideal light evening meal. The honey-toasted sunflower seeds give the salad a wonderful texture – and they also make a great snack on their own. Mimosa is a French culinary term for a combination of spinach and egg.

**MAKES 2 LARGE OR
4 SNACK PORTIONS**

4 large free-range eggs

**125 g/4½ oz/generous 1 cup sunflower
seeds**

Juice of ½ lemon

**30 ml/2 tbsp cold-pressed
virgin olive oil**

**Sea salt and
freshly ground black pepper**

225 g/8 oz baby spinach leaves

15 ml/1 tbsp clear honey

1 Bring a large pan of water to the boil, then gently add the eggs in their shells and simmer for 5–6 minutes. Remove the eggs and cool them slightly under cold running water.

2 Sprinkle the sunflower seeds into a non-stick frying pan (skillet) and toast over a high heat for 2–3 minutes to draw out the natural oil in the seeds. When they are ready, they will turn golden brown.

3 Whisk together the lemon juice, olive oil, salt and pepper to make the dressing. Add the baby spinach leaves and toss gently.

4 Shell the eggs, then grate them into the salad using the coarse side of a grater.

5 Stir the sunflower seeds into the honey.

6 Spoon the salad on to plates, making sure that there is plenty of height and that the salad looks fresh and lively, and sprinkle with the honey-toasted sunflower seeds.

NATURALLY BALANCED Sunflower seeds are an excellent source of calcium and the omega-6 essential fatty acids. This may help to keep your hair, skin and nails healthy, as well as being good for the eyesight. Other sources of omega-6 include sesame, hemp and pumpkin seeds.

Toasted millet grain with peas and mint

Don't make the mistake of thinking that millet grain is just a bird food! It is a gluten-free cereal grain with a delicious nutty taste and texture. What's more, it's extremely cheap and readily available in health food shops.

MAKES 4 PORTIONS

100 ml/3½ fl oz/scant ½ cup cold-pressed virgin olive oil

225 g/8 oz/2 cups millet grain

2.5 ml/½ tsp ground turmeric

2.5 ml/½ tsp ground cumin

5 ml/1 tsp dried mint

600 ml/1 pt/2½ cups vegetable stock

250 g/9 oz thawed frozen peas

1 red (bell) pepper, finely diced

15 ml/1 tbsp chopped fresh mint

Juice of 1 lemon

5 ml/1 tsp unrefined caster (superfine) sugar

Sea salt and freshly ground black pepper

1 Heat a large saucepan, then the add olive oil. When the oil is hot, add the millet, spices and dried mint and fry (sauté) for 4–5 minutes until lightly toasted.

2 Add the vegetable stock and bring to the boil. Reduce the heat, cover and leave to simmer for 25 minutes, stirring occasionally, until all the stock has been absorbed and the grain is light and fluffy. It should have a soft but firm, nutty texture.

3 While the millet is cooking, mix together the peas, pepper, fresh mint, lemon juice and sugar. Leave to marinate until the grain is cooked.

4 Add the cooked grain to the peas and pepper mixture and stir well. Season to taste with a little salt and pepper.

5 Spoon the mixture on to plates and serve warm or cold.

Hints and variations You can add anything you like to this toasted millet grain, such as chopped avocado, cooked chicken or prawns (shrimp). Just follow the same method and omit the dried mint.

Cooked millet grain freezes very well once cooked, so you can prepare it in bulk and then bag or box the cooked grain in the freezer in convenient quantities.

NATURALLY BALANCED When we are under pressure and stressed – which seems to be increasingly the case nowadays – the acid/alkaline balance in our blood level can often become over-acidic, which makes us short-tempered and irritable. Millet is one of the few grains that is alkaline-forming, so redressing this imbalance when it is absorbed into the blood, and making it an extremely beneficial food to be eaten at work for lunch.

Tomato and chilli salad with roasted hazelnuts

Tomato and hazelnuts (filberts) are an excellent combination in terms of both flavour and texture. This salad illustrates just how well they combine – with the help of a little bite of chilli. I prefer to buy tomatoes on the vine as these will usually give you superb flavour and texture and that really makes the difference in this salad.

MAKES 4 PORTIONS

8 vine-ripened tomatoes, coarsely diced

30 ml/2 tbsp hazelnut oil

Juice of ½ lemon

100 g/4 oz/1 cup hazelnuts

1 red chilli, seeded

A pinch of unrefined caster (superfine) sugar

15 ml/1 tbsp chopped fresh coriander (cilantro)

Sea salt and freshly ground black pepper

1 Mix the diced tomatoes with the hazelnut oil and lemon juice and leave to stand.

2 Crush the hazelnuts to a coarse texture using the side of a cook's knife or a pestle and mortar. Place the nuts in a frying pan (skillet) over a high heat for 2–3 minutes until lightly toasted, shaking the pan occasionally. Be careful not to allow the nuts to burn or they may taste slightly bitter.

3 Finely chop the chilli with the pinch of sugar, then add to the tomatoes.

4 Stir in the coriander and crushed hazelnuts and season to taste with salt and pepper.

Serving suggestions This salad combines well with other ingredients such as smoked fish or avocado. You could try it with my Rillette of Avocado (see page 114).

NATURALLY BALANCED Although tomatoes are an acid fruit, they actually turn alkaline after digestion, so can be beneficial for anyone with an over-acidic blood level, which may result from an excess of refined processed foods, stress or toxins in the blood.

Tuna salad with a blue cheese and balsamic dressing

Canned tuna fish is economical, readily available and very good for you. Just check on the label that the tuna has been caught using a dolphin-friendly technique; in the past, dolphins were often dragged up in the tuna nets, which has led to many types becoming endangered species.

MAKES 4 PORTIONS

100 g/4 oz soft blue cheese, such as Cambozola or Dolcelatte

100 ml/3½ fl oz/scant ½ cup plain set Greek yoghurt

15 ml/1 tbsp balsamic vinegar

4 spring onions (scallions), chopped

1 garlic clove, crushed

Sea salt

A little cayenne

1 x 185 g/6½ oz/small can of flaked tuna in water, drained

1 head of cos or little gem lettuce, cut into large cubes

Juice of ½ lemon

100 g/4 oz/1 cup roasted salted cashew nuts, coarsely crushed

1 Purée the cheese, yoghurt, balsamic vinegar, spring onions and garlic in a liquidiser or food processor. Season to taste with salt and cayenne.

2 Mix together the tuna and lettuce, then spike with the lemon juice.

3 Add a good spoonful of the blue cheese dressing and half the crushed cashew nuts and gently mix together.

4 Spoon into individual salad bowls, sprinkle with the remaining cashew nuts and serve a little extra blue cheese dressing on the side.

Hints and variations If you are using a food processor, it is easier to make a large batch of blue cheese dressing. You can store it in the fridge for at least a week and it will go well with most salads, meats and fish dishes.

NATURALLY BALANCED Fresh tuna is rich in the omega-3 fatty acids found in oily fish, but this is lost in the canning process, although the mineral selenium is retained. Selenium is an anti-oxidant that is vital for the metabolism of the cells in the body. This mineral also helps the body deal with alcohol and toxic products, such as smoke and many fats.

Red cabbage, caraway and ricotta stir-fry salad

*Stir-frying is a method that cooks quickly and with the minimum of oil, which means
that the ingredients retain much of their energy and nutritional value. It is suitable for
almost every kind of ingredient, so don't save it just for oriental dishes. I use sunflower
oil for stir-frying and walnut oil to finish this dish.*

MAKES 4 PORTIONS

100 g/4 oz/1 cup walnuts,
coarsely crushed

½ medium red cabbage,
quartered and cored

15 ml/1 tbsp sunflower oil

5 ml/1 tsp caraway seeds

1 red onion, sliced

2 cooking (tart) apples, cored, cut in
half and thinly sliced

30 ml/2 tbsp balsamic vinegar

5 ml/1 tsp muscovado sugar

Sea salt and
freshly ground black pepper

100 g/4 oz/½ cup ricotta cheese

30 ml/2 tbsp walnut oil

1 Put the crushed walnuts into a wok or deep frying pan (skillet) and
place over a high heat for 3–4 minutes until lightly toasted, stirring all
the time so that the walnuts don't burn on the base of the pan.
Remove the walnuts from the pan.

2 Coarsely slice the cabbage either with a sharp knife or with a food
processor. If you are cutting by hand, make sure the slices are not
too chunky.

3 Add the sunflower oil to the pan, then throw in the toasted walnuts
and the caraway seeds and stir-fry for 1 minute. Now add the red
cabbage and onion and continue to cook for 2 minutes.

4 Just before you turn off the heat, stir in the apples.

5 Mix together the balsamic vinegar, sugar and a touch of salt and
pepper and stir well, then add to the pan.

6 Remove the pan from the heat. Gently fold in half the walnuts and all
the ricotta.

7 Spoon the stir-fry into individual bowls and sprinkle with the
remaining walnuts and the walnut oil.

Serving suggestion This salad is perfect as a side dish to any main
course. I like it with my Venison Steaks with Orange, Prunes and
Cinnamon (see page 122).

NATURALLY BALANCED Cabbage, especially red cabbage, is laden with
vitamin C. There is more to this vitamin than we often think – it is needed to
make collagen and it's essential for strengthening many parts of the body,
such as muscles and blood vessels. It also aids in the formation of liver bile
and may help to fight viruses and to detoxify alcohol and other substances.

Wild rice salad with fennel and orange

Wild rice – which is actually a type of grass – remains the staple food of the Native Americans. It has a unique flavour and texture, which in this recipe is perked up with the liveliness of fresh orange. Wild rice is inexpensive and easy to cook. It is available in large supermarkets and health food shops.

MAKES 4 PORTIONS

225 g/8 oz/1 cup wild rice, soaked in cold water for 1 hour

750 ml/1¼ pts/3 cups vegetable stock

5 ml/1 tsp fennel seeds

2 eating (dessert) apples, cored

1 medium fennel bulb

125 g/4½ oz/generous 1 cup flaked (slivered) almonds

30 ml/2 tbsp sultanas (golden raisins)

30 ml/2 tbsp hazelnut (filbert) or cold-pressed virgin olive oil

15 ml/1 tbsp balsamic vinegar

Grated zest and juice of 1 orange

Sea salt and freshly ground black pepper

1 Drain and rinse the wild rice with cold water. Pour into a saucepan and add the vegetable stock and fennel seeds. Bring to the boil, then reduce the heat and simmer, uncovered, for 35–40 minutes until just tender. You can speed up this process by using a pressure cooker, which will take just 10 minutes once the pan reaches pressure.

2 Meanwhile, cut the apples and fennel into thin slices and mix with half the almonds and all the remaining ingredients in a mixing bowl.

3 Drain the rice well, then combine it with the other ingredients and mix well, seasoning to taste with salt and pepper.

4 Spoon into individual bowls or a large serving dish and sprinkle with the remaining almonds.

Hints and variations You can combine the same ingredients with other types of rice and there are many to choose from. Try introducing your family to different varieties and see which they prefer.

All cooked rice freezes very well and therefore can be stored, ready for use. Just remove from the freezer the night before to allow it to defrost completely.

NATURALLY BALANCED Wild rice contains lots of protein and is packed full of essential minerals and B-vitamins. This makes wild rice a perfect superfood for anyone who leads an active or physically demanding life!

Quinoa grain pilaff

Quinoa was regarded as a sacred grain by the Inca and Maya tribes of South America, who praised its supernatural powers. You will find this 'wonder' grain in most health food shops or large supermarkets.
See photograph opposite page 72.

MAKES 4 PORTIONS

15 ml/1 tbsp sunflower oil

1 onion, finely chopped

5 ml/1 tsp medium curry powder

200 g/7 oz/1¾ cups quinoa grain

750 ml/1¼ pts/3 cups vegetable stock, made with 1 stock cube

15 ml/1 tbsp chopped fresh parsley

Juice of ½ lemon

Sea salt and freshly ground black pepper

1 Heat the oil in a saucepan, add the onion and cook for 1 minute until the onion is transparent, then stir in the curry powder.

2 Add the quinoa and continue to cook for a few minutes until the grains absorb the spices, stirring continuously.

3 Add the stock and bring to a rapid boil. Add a pinch of salt, reduce the heat slightly, and allow the quinoa to cook, uncovered, for 14–16 minutes. You will know when the grain is ready as sprouts will start to pop out of the grain and the stock will have been absorbed.

4 Stir in the parsley and lemon juice and season to taste with salt and pepper.

5 Tip into individual bowls or a large serving dish and serve hot or cold.

Serving suggestions Serve this pilaff with dishes such as my Moroccan Chickpea and Coriander Casserole (see page 74) or as a side dish with your favourite meat or fish.

Hints and variations Quinoa grain is lovely mixed with cooked pulses and chopped raw vegetables. It makes an excellent energy-boosting lunchtime salad.

NATURALLY BALANCED This supergrain is at least as good as meat and fish as a source of essential amino acids. Quinoa is extremely versatile and is also gluten-free, making it ideal for the increasing number of people avoiding this product. The grain can grow in extremely dry conditions and also does not appear to sap the soil of vital nutrients.

food for the FAMILY

Family meals are a special time when you not only feed your family's bodies but also nourish their togetherness. The ingredients you use should be easy to find, economical and accessible, and the dishes quick and easy to prepare, nutritious and filling – and that's what I've achieved with this great batch of recipes. Many of the dishes can be adapted to suit the different requirements of family members. For example, you can be bold or subtle with strong spices such as cayenne and garlic, depending on your family's likes and dislikes. Don't leave them out entirely – just tone down the flavour so that no one complains! You will find that many of the dishes in this section can be made in advance and frozen ready for days when you're short of time. Providing they are only stored for a short time, this will not impair the flavour or nutritional content.

Baked savoury bread pudding with herbs and cheese

It always used to annoy my mother when I was young that I often opened up a new packet of cheese before the old one was eaten. If that happens in your house, try keeping the trimmings and odd bits of cheese in a well-sealed freezer bag in the freezer until you have enough to make this wonderfully wholesome bread pudding.

MAKES 4 PORTIONS

50 g/2 oz/¼ cup salted butter

1 onion, finely chopped

5 ml/1 tsp dried mixed herbs

200 g/7 oz button mushrooms, wiped and sliced

A little cayenne

Sea salt and freshly ground black pepper

3 large free-range eggs, beaten

300 ml/½ pt/1¼ cups milk

5 ml/1 tsp Dijon mustard

1 bunch of spring onions (scallions), finely chopped

8 slices of wholemeal or white bread, crusts removed

225 g/8 oz/2 cups hard cheese, grated

1 Preheat the oven to 190°C/375°F/gas 5/fan oven 170°C and grease a deep ovenproof dish.

2 Melt the butter in a large sauté pan or frying pan (skillet), then add the onion and herbs and cook over a gentle heat for about 3 minutes until the onions are soft and transparent.

3 Add the mushrooms and cook for a further 3 minutes, stirring to coat them in the butter.

4 Remove from the heat and season with cayenne, salt and pepper.

5 Whisk together the eggs, milk and mustard, then stir in the spring onions and season lightly with salt and pepper.

6 Arrange half the bread slices over the prepared dish. Spoon over the cooked mushrooms, then sprinkle with half the cheese. Cover with the remaining bread, then top with the remaining cheese and gently pour the milk mixture over the top.

7 Place the dish on a baking (cookie) tray and cook in the preheated oven for 30–35 minutes until cooked through and golden on top.

Serving suggestions As this dish already contains starch, I would recommend serving just two simple salads with it. You could try my Tomato and Chilli Salad (see page 27) and either Oriental or Caribbean Coleslaw (see pages 22 and 23).

NATURALLY BALANCED I like to use free-range, organic, locally sourced eggs. Standard commercial battery eggs are laid by hens that live in sterile, mechanical environments and are fed various drugs as part of their normal feeding regime. Their eggs are often deficient in vitamin B12 and are lacking in virtually every other nutrient that eggs should contain. Folklore maintains that the unhappiness of the hen is passed on through her eggs.

Caribbean macaroni pie

This tasty and economical dish is a number one favourite with the locals on the beautiful island of Barbados, although their version is much hotter!

MAKES 6 PORTIONS

500 g/1¼ lb macaroni

1 bunch of spring onions (scallions), finely chopped

Grated zest and juice of 1 lemon

60 ml/4 tbsp tomato ketchup (catsup)

1 red chilli, seeded and finely chopped

200 ml/7 fl oz/scant 1 cup full-fat plain Greek yoghurt

15 ml/1 tbsp Dijon mustard

15 ml/1 tbsp Worcestershire sauce

A pinch of cayenne

Sea salt and freshly ground black pepper

Chilli powder (optional)

FOR THE TOPPING

100 g/4 oz/1 cup hard cheese, grated

100 g/4 oz/1 cup dried breadcrumbs

15 ml/1 tbsp chopped fresh parsley

5 ml/1 tsp paprika

1 Preheat the oven to 200°C/400°F/gas 6/fan oven 180°C.

2 Grease a large ovenproof dish and stand it on a baking (cookie) tray.

3 Bring a large pan of lightly salted water to the boil, add the macaroni and return to the boil. Boil for about 10 minutes, or as directed on the packet, until just tender. Drain well.

4 Place the pasta in a large bowl, add all the other main ingredients except the lemon zest and mix together, seasoning to taste with cayenne, salt and pepper.

5 Stir in a little chilli powder, if liked, then transfer to the prepared baking dish. If you want to make only half the dish hot, spoon half the pasta mixture into one half of the prepared baking dish, then spice up the remainder before transferring it to the dish.

6 Mix all the topping ingredients with the lemon zest, and season to taste with more cayenne and a little salt. Sprinkle this mixture over the macaroni.

7 Bake in the preheated oven for 35–40 minutes until the topping is golden brown and crunchy. You can serve it straight away, but if the family aren't ready for dinner, you can turn off the oven and leave the pie keeping warm for about 30 minutes.

Serving suggestions This dish is ideal served with a seasonal salad tossed in a simple dressing (try the one on page 127) and perhaps some warm bread.

Hints and variations If you are making one side of the dish really hot and the other mild, do remember to mark which end is which!

If you want to make the pie in advance, it will keep well in the fridge for up to two days, then you can reheat it in a medium oven for 15–20 minutes until piping hot throughout and crisp on top.

NATURALLY BALANCED Try not to eat too much pasta or other starchy ingredients very late at night, as these are glutinous foods that require a lot of energy to digest at a time when your digestive system is meant to be resting. This can lead to interrupted sleep and loss of appetite for breakfast the next morning, which in turn can make you feel tired and lethargic later in the day.

Leek and cheddar cheese clafoutis with garlic

Clafoutis is a traditional French dessert consisting of a sweet batter baked with fruits. I have taken the basic components of clafoutis and made them into this easy-to-prepare savoury dish. It makes a perfect evening meal for informal entertaining, especially warming on a beautiful autumn or winter evening.

MAKES 4 PORTIONS

4 large free-range eggs

500 ml/17 fl oz/2¼ cups milk

30 ml/2 tbsp unbleached plain (all-purpose) flour

10 ml/2 tsp Dijon mustard

Cayenne

Sea salt

2–3 medium leeks

50 g/2 oz/¼ cup salted butter

3 garlic cloves, crushed

1 bunch of fresh chives, finely snipped

150 g/5 oz/1¼ cups mature Cheddar cheese, coarsely grated

1 Preheat the oven to 200°C/400°F/gas 6/fan oven 180°C.

2 Whisk together the eggs, milk, flour, mustard and a pinch each of cayenne and salt, then leave to stand for 10 minutes.

3 Wash the leeks very thoroughly under cold running water to remove any grit, and shred finely.

4 Heat a large saucepan, then add the butter, leeks and garlic and cook over a gentle heat for 7–8 minutes until soft, stirring occasionally. Season with a little cayenne and salt.

5 Spoon the leeks into a greased ovenproof dish, then pour over the egg mixture and sprinkle with the chives and cheese.

6 Bake in the preheated oven for 25–30 minutes until the clafoutis is golden brown and puffed up – although it will sink back down when you remove it from the oven. Serve straight from the baking dish.

Serving suggestions As this dish contains all the ingredients for a meal in itself, the best accompaniment is a crisp green salad and some crunchy bread.

Hints and variations You can use any filling you like, but the combination of leeks with cheese and garlic marries very well – and is also very economical. You can even use the chopped leftovers from the previous night's supper. I like to use a strong mature Cheddar, but you can use whatever hard cheese you prefer. Another option is to cook the dish in individual ramekin dishes, particularly if you are entertaining.

NATURALLY BALANCED Studies suggest that eating garlic regularly may reduce the risk of cancers of the oesophagus, stomach and colon. This is believed to be partly due to garlic's ability to reduce the formation of carcinogenic compounds.

South american kidney bean pulao

Pulao is a South American word used to describe a stew. This is an interesting vegetable dish in which the rice is cooked in one dish with all the other ingredients. The various exotic spices, such as cinnamon and cardamom, give off a most wonderful aroma.

MAKES 4–6 PORTIONS

225 g/8 oz/1 cup basmati rice

15 ml/1 tbsp sunflower oil

1 cinnamon stick

2 cloves, crushed

2 green cardamom pods, crushed

10 ml/2 tsp curry powder

1 onion, thinly sliced

100 g/4 oz frozen peas

2 courgettes (zucchini), sliced

1 cauliflower, cut into small florets

1 x 225 g/8 oz/small can of red kidney beans, rinsed and drained

600 ml/1 pt/2½ cups vegetable stock

Juice of ½ lemon

Sea salt

15 ml/1 tbsp chopped fresh coriander (cilantro)

1 Put the rice in a bowl and cover with cold water. Leave to soak while you prepare the remaining ingredients.

2 Heat a large saucepan, add the oil and heat gently. Add the cinnamon stick, cloves, cardamom pods and curry powder and mix together. Add the onion and sauté gently for 1 minute.

3 Add the peas, courgettes and cauliflower and cook gently for 2 minutes, stirring occasionally.

4 Drain the rice, then add it to the pan with the kidney beans and stock. Increase the heat and bring to the boil, then reduce the heat, cover and leave to simmer for about 10 minutes, stirring occasionally, until all the liquid has been absorbed and the rice is tender.

5 Remove the cinnamon stick, then stir in the lemon juice and season to taste with salt.

6 Spoon into a warmed serving bowl and sprinkle with the coriander.

Serving suggestions You can serve the pulao hot with a delicious side dish such as Caribbean Coleslaw (see page 23) and warm, crusty bread. Alternatively, leave it to cool and serve it as a salad, or even take it to work as a packed lunch dish and make all your colleagues envious!

NATURALLY BALANCED Rice and pulses make a valuable food combination. Eaten together, these two ingredients provide all the essential amino acids that help with the constant rebuilding of cells in the body.

Five-colour vegetable stir-fry with roasted cashews

This dish, with its contrasts of colours and textures, looks and tastes wonderful and is simplicity itself to prepare. The aroma of the nuts as they cook is quite sensational.

MAKES 4–6 PORTIONS

100 g/4 oz/1 cup roasted and salted cashew nuts

15 ml/1 tbsp sesame oil

1 onion, thinly sliced

1 red (bell) pepper, thinly sliced

2 carrots, peeled and cut into thin strips

100 g/4 oz broccoli, cut into small florets

1 cm/½ in piece of fresh root ginger, peeled and finely grated

100 g/4 oz shiitake mushrooms

1 x 225 g/8 oz/small can of bamboo shoots, drained

45 ml/3 tbsp soy sauce

Juice of ½ lemon

A pinch of unrefined caster (superfine) sugar

1 bunch of fresh coriander (cilantro), finely chopped

1 Crush the cashew nuts with a mortar and pestle or the side of a large knife.

2 Place a wok or large frying pan (skillet) on the highest heat until the pan is hot.

3 Add the sesame oil and heat for a few seconds, then add the onion and pepper and stir-fry for 30 seconds.

4 Add the carrots and broccoli and stir-fry for 2 minutes.

5 Add the ginger, mushrooms, bamboo shoots, soy sauce, lemon juice and sugar and stir-fry for 1 minute.

6 Add half the crushed cashew nuts and mix together well.

7 Spoon the stir-fry, with its juices, on to individual plates and sprinkle with the remaining cashew nuts and the coriander.

Serving suggestions This is delicious on its own – or just serve it with a crisp salad or noodles.

Hints and variations The key to successful stir-frying is speed. Have everything prepared before you start to cook, chopping the vegetables at the last minute to help maintain their optimum vitality levels. Get the wok nice and hot, use only a little oil and don't leave the vegetables in the pan for too long. Follow these tips and the stir-fry will be fresh, crisp and nutritiously delicious!

It is best to crush the cashew nuts for this dish rather than chop them, as this will help to release their wonderful aroma.

You can add prawns (shrimp) or thinly sliced chicken or beef to the dish to make it even more substantial. Simple toss your chosen ingredients in the wok until cooked through and hot, then remove from the wok and keep warm while you make the stir-fry, adding them back into the pan with the cashew nuts.

NATURALLY BALANCED Shiitake mushrooms are known to be a good source of germanium, an element that improves cellular oxygenation and enhances immunity. They are also believed to be a natural source of interferon, a protein that appears to induce an immune response against cancer and viral infections.

Mushroom and apricot cassoulet with herbs

A cassoulet is a French casserole, usually made with pork, lamb and pulses. This delicious meatless version is just as warming and flavoursome, and the apricots and spices add an extra special touch.

MAKES 6 PORTIONS

100 ml/3½ fl oz/scant ½ cup boiling water

100 g/4 oz/⅔ cup dried unsulphured apricots

30 ml/2 tbsp sunflower oil

2 onions, finely chopped

5 ml/1 tsp dried mixed herbs

2 bay leaves

1 cinnamon stick

5 ml/1 tsp ground cumin

2.5 ml/½ tsp ground cloves

2 garlic cloves, crushed

100 g/4 oz button mushrooms, sliced

Sea salt

15 ml/1 tbsp tomato purée (paste)

1 x 225 g/8 oz/small can of red kidney beans, drained

1 x 225 g/8 oz/small can of butter (lima) beans, drained

1 x 225 g/8 oz/small can of chopped tomatoes

500 ml/17 fl oz/2¼ cups vegetable stock

A little cayenne

1 Pour the boiling water over the apricots and leave to soak.

2 Heat a large saucepan or flameproof casserole dish (Dutch oven) and add the oil. Once hot, add the onions, dried herbs and spices and sauté for 2–3 minutes, stirring regularly.

3 Add the garlic, mushrooms and a good pinch of salt and continue to sauté for a further 2 minutes.

4 Add the tomato purée and both cans of beans and cook for a further 4 minutes, stirring well so that the purée does not stick to the bottom of the pan.

5 Drain the apricots and finely chop them, then add to the pan with the tomatoes and stock. Bring to the boil, then reduce the heat and simmer for 14–16 minutes, uncovered, stirring occasionally. The cassoulet will have thickened slightly.

6 Remove the cinnamon stick and add a pinch of cayenne and more salt, if needed.

7 Transfer to a large serving dish, spoon over the yoghurt and sprinkle with the parsley.

TO FINISH

120 ml/4 fl oz/½ cup plain set Greek yoghurt

30 ml/2 tbsp chopped fresh parsley

Serving suggestions I would suggest a grain side dish such as my Roasted Spiced Couscous (see page 18) or Quinoa Grain Pilaff (see page 31). A simple green salad and warm bread perfectly complement such a hearty dish.

Hints and variations All the ingredients for this vegetable dish can be kept in the kitchen cupboard for several months. Once made up, the dish will keep hot without spoiling for a long time, making it ideal for the family to tuck into if they eat at different times. It also freezes well.

NATURALLY BALANCED The chemical lycopene, which is related to the pigment in tomatoes, has now been proved to help strengthen the heart and arteries. Interestingly, though, it has been shown that more lycopene is absorbed into the body when the tomatoes are cooked. Many biomedical researchers believe that lycopene may also help reduce the risk of certain cancers.

Traditional spanish tortilla

This dish can be found in different guises all over Spain. It is a very useful and creative way of using up leftover potatoes and is always a big favourite with the family. in fact, it is so popular I know some people who cook potatoes especially for the dish!

MAKES 4 PORTIONS

300 g/11 oz raw or cooked potatoes, diced

15 ml/1 tbsp cold-pressed virgin olive oil

2 onions, sliced

1 garlic clove, crushed

Sea salt and freshly ground black pepper

6 large free-range eggs

30 ml/2 tbsp milk

1 Preheat the oven to 200°C/400°F/gas 6/fan oven 180°C.

2 If you are using raw potatoes, put them in a saucepan and add just enough water to cover. Bring to the boil, then reduce the heat and simmer for 7–8 minutes until tender. Drain well.

3 Heat a large non-stick frying pan (skillet) – it must be suitable for placing in the oven – and add the olive oil. Once hot, add the onions and sauté gently for 2–3 minutes.

4 Add the crushed garlic and season with salt and pepper, then add the cooked potatoes and continue to sauté gently for 2 minutes, making sure that all the ingredients are well mixed together.

5 Beat the eggs with the milk and a little salt and pepper, then pour into the frying pan. Cook for about 1 minute to colour one side of the tortilla.

6 Place the pan in the oven for 14 minutes to cook the whole omelette. To test if it is ready, press the middle with your finger – it should be firm to the touch but still soft.

7 Remove from the oven and loosen the omelette around the outside of the pan with a plastic spatula if necessary. Place a warm serving plate on top, then quickly invert the pan, turning out the tortilla to serve on the plate.

Serving suggestions Because this tortilla contains potatoes, it's very substantial, so I would serve it with just a simple salad or vegetables as a side dish and perhaps some warm bread.

NATURALLY BALANCED It is recommended that we should eat only two or three eggs per week. Always try to buy fresh eggs from free-range hens. These contain more beneficial nutrients and flavour than battery hens' eggs.

Buckwheat savoury pancakes

Buckwheat flour has an earthy but delicate, sweet taste and it speckles the batter with attractive tiny flecks. Using this flour gives a subtle but deliciously different taste to pancakes.

MAKES 8 LARGE PANCAKES

150 ml/¼ pt/⅔ cup milk

150 ml/¼ pt/⅔ cup water

1 large free-range egg

50 g/2 oz/¹/₂ cup buckwheat flour

90 g/3¹/₂ oz/scant ¹/₂ cup unbleached plain (all-purpose) flour

2.5 ml/½ tsp sea salt

A pinch of freshly ground black pepper

25 g/1 oz/2 tbsp salted butter, melted

1 To make the batter, whisk together all the ingredients except the melted butter in a bowl until smooth, or blend in a liquidiser or processor, scraping down the sides halfway through if necessary.

2 Heat a small non-stick frying pan (skillet) and brush with some of the melted butter.

3 Pour in just enough batter to coat the pan lightly, and rotate the pan to spread the batter evenly over the base. Cook for a few minutes until the pancake begins to become dry around the edges.

4 Carefully loosen around the edges with a spatula and turn the pancake over. Cook for a further minute on the other side, then remove the pancake from the pan and keep it warm while you cook the remaining pancakes in the same way. Serve hot.

Serving suggestions Buckwheat pancakes with a savoury stuffing make a perfect meal. Try filling them with Mushroom Fricassee (see page 67) or even Sag Aloo (see page 84). If you are serving them as a main course, accompany them with a crisp green salad. Of course, you can also serve them as a snack or a dessert, just with a little lemon juice and sugar or honey.

Hints and variations Buckwheat has an enormous capacity to absorb water, so you may find it necessary to thin the batter with more water or milk if it has rested for some time. The first pancake quite often does not work but turns into a soggy mess in the pan. Take heart if this happens – just throw it away and proceed to the next one!

NATURALLY BALANCED Buckwheat is a good source of the bioflavonoid rutin. This substance may help to strengthen capillaries and blood vessels, reduce blood pressure and assist circulation to the hands and feet.

Tagliatelle of salmon and parmesan with chilli

Though most people already have their favourite pasta dishes, I hope this dish helps to give you some useful tips for other pasta ideas. The fennel helps cool the heat of the chilli and the chilli helps break the richness of the salmon. I like to use wholewheat pasta, but you can use any type you prefer.

MAKES 4 PORTIONS

450 g/1 lb tagliatelle

350–400 g/12–14 oz salmon fillet, skinned and boned

A pinch of fennel seeds (optional)

Sea salt and freshly ground black pepper

60 ml/4 tbsp cold-pressed virgin olive oil

2 garlic cloves, crushed

1 medium fennel bulb, coarsely grated

1 red or green chilli, seeded and finely chopped

Juice of 2 lemons

1 small bunch of fresh chives, finely snipped

100 g/4 oz/1 cup freshly grated Parmesan cheese

1 Bring a large pan of lightly salted water to the boil, add the pasta and cook until just tender, according to the instructions on the packet.

2 While the pasta is cooking, cut the salmon into bite-sized pieces and season with fennel seeds, if using, and salt and pepper.

3 Heat a large frying pan (skillet), then add half of the olive oil and heat. Add the salmon and the crushed garlic and sauté for 2–3 minutes until the pieces are just sealed.

4 Add the grated fennel and chopped chilli and continue to cook for a further 2 minutes, stirring gently so as not to break up the salmon too much.

5 Meanwhile, drain the pasta and place back in the hot saucepan, turn off the heat and pour the remaining olive oil into the pasta. Add the cooked salmon, fennel and chilli, followed by the lemon juice and half the chives.

6 Transfer to a large serving dish and sprinkle with the Parmesan and remaining chives.

Serving suggestions This needs nothing more than a simple green salad.

Hints and variations You can replace the salmon with prawns (shrimp) or finely diced chicken. If you are using raw chicken, make sure you cook it for at least 10 minutes before adding it to the pasta. It is also good cold, so you can pop any leftovers into lunch boxes.

NATURALLY BALANCED Refined white pasta is known to slow down the metabolism if eaten too often. When planning menus at home, aim to have pasta just once a week for dinner. If the family enjoy wholewheat pasta, then switch to that. You can now get all types of unrefined pasta in health food shops and good supermarkets.

Meatloaf with almonds and ginger

I think meatloaf is underrated; it makes an excellent, inexpensive meal, both hot and cold. If you think it sounds a bit dull, then try this recipe – the apricots, almonds and porridge oats all help to add a unique flavour and texture.

MAKES 1 x 900 G/2 LB LOAF (ABOUT 6 PORTIONS)

600 g/1 lb 6 oz lean minced (ground) pork

200 g/7 oz lean minced beef

75 g/3 oz/½ cup dried unsulphured apricots, roughly chopped

2 onions, quartered

100 g/4 oz/1 cup flaked (slivered) almonds

50 g/2 oz/½ cup rolled porridge oats

15 ml/1 tbsp tomato purée (paste)

15 ml/1 tbsp Worcestershire sauce

1 large free-range egg, beaten

2.5 cm/1 in piece of fresh root ginger, peeled and finely grated

5 ml/1 tsp dried mixed herbs

2.5 ml/½ tsp ground cumin

A little sea salt

A pinch of cayenne

1 Preheat the oven to 190°C/375°F/gas 5/fan oven 170°C. Grease and line a 900 g/2 lb loaf tin (pan) and stand it on a baking (cookie) tray.

2 Finely chop the meats, apricots and onions in a food processor, then transfer to a large mixing bowl.

3 Reserve half the flaked almonds, then add all the remaining ingredients to the bowl and season with a little salt and cayenne. Mix well.

4 Gently press the mixture into the prepared loaf tin and pat down evenly. The mixture will shrink slightly once cooked so don't worry if the tin looks too full. Sprinkle the reserved almonds over the top of the loaf and bake in the preheated oven for 1 hour. You will know when the meatloaf is almost done as it will start to come away from the sides of the tin.

5 Turn the meatloaf out on to a warmed serving plate.

Serving suggestions For a substantial hot meal, serve with Simple Creamy Mashed Potatoes (see page 101), fresh vegetables and Caramelised Onion Sauce (see page 124). It is also delicious cold, sliced, in a sandwich with chutney and salad.

Hints and variations If you want to freeze the meatloaf, leave it to cool in the tin, then remove, wrap and freeze for up to one month. To reheat, simply defrost the meatloaf overnight in its original tin, then place in a preheated medium oven for 20 minutes to reheat thoroughly.

NATURALLY BALANCED Ginger is an excellent aid to digestion, particularly when served with meat. Indigestion can be caused simply by eating too fast, so do try not to rush your meals. If you do suffer from indigestion, try crushing a small piece of fresh ginger with a slice of lemon and a teaspoon of honey in boiling water for a refreshing after-meal infusion.

Chilli con carne with cocoa

In certain parts of Mexico and South America, cocoa (unsweetened chocolate) powder is an essential ingredient in many savoury dishes, and it helps produce a unique flavour and richness in the finished dish.

MAKES 4–6 PORTIONS

30 ml/2 tbsp sunflower or groundnut (peanut) oil

3 onions, chopped

500 g/18 oz lean minced (ground) beef

3 garlic cloves, crushed

10 ml/2 tsp cocoa powder

5 ml/1 tsp unbleached plain (all-purpose) flour

2.5 ml/½ tsp dried chilli flakes

A good pinch of cayenne

5 ml/1 tsp sea salt

Freshly ground black pepper

1 x 225 g/8 oz/small can of red kidney beans, drained

1 large or 2 small green (bell) peppers, chopped

30 ml/2 tbsp tomato purée (paste)

600 ml/1 pt/2½ cups vegetable stock

100 ml/3½ fl oz/scant 1 cup soured (dairy sour) cream

15 ml/1 tbsp chopped fresh parsley

1 Heat a large saucepan, add the oil and heat gently. Stir in the onions and leave to cook for about 2 minutes until transparent.

2 Meanwhile, place the mince in a bowl and mix in the garlic, cocoa, flour, chilli flakes, cayenne, salt and plenty of pepper.

3 Increase the heat under the pan, add the mince and stir until the mince is well coloured. Make sure that the pan is hot enough to brown the meat quickly. If the pan starts to lose heat, remove the ingredients and clean the pan. Replace on the stove with a little more oil, heat again, then reintroduce the mixture a little at a time.

4 Add the kidney beans, peppers, tomato purée and stock. Stir well and bring to the boil. Reduce the heat, cover with a tight-fitting lid and simmer gently for 20–25 minutes, stirring every 10 minutes or so.

5 Taste and adjust the seasoning if necessary, then transfer to a warm serving dish. Spoon the soured cream over the top and sprinkle with the chopped parsley to give an attractive finish.

Serving suggestions Chilli con Carne is undoubtedly best served with rice, so try my Fluffy Basmati Rice (see page 88). Alternatively, serve it with Simple Creamy Mashed Potatoes (see page 101). Accompany with fresh seasonal vegetables or a green salad.

Hints and variations You can easily make a vegetarian version of this chilli by using minced Quorn or other meat substitute, and you can adjust the heat of the chilli to suit your own taste, especially if your family includes young children.

NATURALLY BALANCED It is best to avoid the cheaper brands of minced meat, as they are often bulked out with large quantities of excess fat and gristle. It is always worth the extra few pennies that top-grade minced beef costs – you'll get an excellent flavour and peace of mind!

Banana and rum torte with peaches

*I always find that desserts help everyone feel satisfied and content and this is a really
hearty and economical dessert for all the family to enjoy. The recipe is very simple but
impressive and makes good use of storecupboard ingredients.*

MAKES 6–8 PORTIONS

FOR THE FILLING

1 x 225 g/8 oz/small can of peaches in
natural juice, drained

2 bananas, peeled and sliced

30 ml/2 tbsp dark rum

Grated zest and juice of 1 orange

FOR THE BASE

125 g/4½ oz/generous 1 cup ground
almonds

100 g/4 oz/1 cup unbleached plain
(all-purpose) flour

50 g/2 oz/¼ cup muscovado sugar

100 g/4 oz/½ cup salted butter

15 ml/1 tbsp cold water

FOR THE TOPPING

100 g/4 oz/½ cup salted butter

100 g/4 oz/½ cup unbleached plain
(all-purpose) flour

100 g/4 oz/½ cup muscovado sugar

50 g/2 oz/½ cup flaked (slivered)
almonds

5 ml/1 tsp ground cinnamon

1 Preheat the oven to 190°C/375°F/gas 5/fan oven 170°C and grease
a shallow 20 cm/8 in flan tin (pie pan).

2 Mix together the peaches, bananas, rum and orange zest and juice
in a bowl and leave to one side to marinate.

3 To make the base, blend the ground almonds, flour, sugar, butter
and water in a food processor until holding together. Alternatively,
rub the butter into the dry ingredients in a bowl, then bind together
with the water.

4 Press the mixture into the prepared flan tin and spread the peach
and banana mixture over the base.

5 To prepare the topping, rub the butter into the flour, sugar, almonds
and cinnamon until the mixture resembles fine breadcrumbs.
Sprinkle the topping over the fruit filling.

6 Bake in the preheated oven for 40–45 minutes until golden on top.

7 Serve from the baking tin, as it is extremely delicate when baked.

Serving suggestions Serve with dollops of thick plain yoghurt or
clotted cream.

Hints and variations This torte freezes very well, and can be
defrosted and then reheated in a hot oven for about 15 minutes.

NATURALLY BALANCED In Eastern medicine, almonds are believed to build
an essence known as *ojas*, which is thought to increase the intellect and
reproductive ability!

Baked chocolate pudding

Although this is chocolate heaven, it will not break your household food budget as the recipe uses cocoa (unsweetened chocolate) powder instead of block chocolate. Warming and slightly gooey without being sickly, it is fabulous served with cream on the side on a cold and wet winter evening.

MAKES 4–6 PORTIONS

100 g/4 oz/½ cup unsalted (sweet) butter, melted

75 g/3 oz/¾ cup cocoa powder

175 g/6 oz/1½ cups unbleached plain (all-purpose) flour

100 g/4 oz/1 cup dried milk powder (non-fat dry milk)

10 ml/2 tsp baking powder

75 g/3 oz/⅓ cup refined caster (superfine) sugar

A pinch of sea salt

5 ml/1 tsp vanilla essence (extract)

100 ml/3½ fl oz/scant ½ cup cold water

225 g/8 oz/1 cup muscovado sugar

400 ml/14 fl oz/1¾ cups boiling water

1 Preheat the oven to 180°C/350°F/gas 4/fan oven 160°C and use 40 g/1½ oz/3 tbsp of the butter to grease a shallow 20 cm/8 in ovenproof dish.

2 Reserve 15 ml/1 tbsp of the cocoa, then mix the remainder with the flour, dried milk, baking powder, sugar and salt in a bowl.

3 Add the remaining melted butter, the vanilla essence and the cold water and mix to a stiff batter. Pour into the prepared dish.

4 Mix together the muscovado sugar with the reserved cocoa and sprinkle over the top of the pudding, then pour over the boiling water. Bake in the preheated oven for about 45 minutes until risen and just firm to the touch.

Serving suggestions Serve with double (heavy) cream, ice cream or plain Greek yoghurt.

Hints and variations To make this dessert dairy-free and suitable for vegans, change the dried milk to soya powder, use dairy-free margarine instead of butter, and add an extra 100 g/4 oz/½ cup of sugar to the batter (you need this as there is no lactose sugar in soya powder).

NATURALLY BALANCED Hyperactivity can often indicate a blood sugar overload. While it is a treat to eat a sugary dessert, we must also be cautious of the corrosive effect that sugar has on the body and blood balance.

Photograph opposite: Baked Potatoes with a Twist (see page 20) and Spinach Mimosa Salad with Toasted Sunflower Seeds (see page 25).

Apple and ginger crumble with oats and muscovado

My special topping gives a distinctive taste and texture to a traditional crumble. The apple and ginger underneath provide a simple but warming combination, but you can use any fruit you like.

MAKES 4–6 PORTIONS

6 cooking (tart) apples, peeled, cored and chopped

15 ml/1 tbsp muscovado sugar

2.5 cm/1 in piece of fresh root ginger, peeled and finely grated

Juice of ½ lemon

A pinch of ground cinnamon

A pinch of ground ginger

FOR THE CRUMBLE
100 g/4 oz/1 cup unbleached plain (all-purpose) flour

100 g/4 oz/1 cup rolled porridge oats

100 g/4 oz/½ cup muscovado sugar

100 g/4 oz/½ cup salted butter

**Photograph opposite:
Giant Burgers (see page 55) in
Home-made Burger Buns (see page 54)
with Home-made Oven-baked Chips
(see page 56).**

1 Preheat the oven to 190°C/375°F/gas 5/fan oven 170°C and lightly grease a deep 25 cm/10 in ovenproof dish.

2 Mix together the apples, sugar, ginger, lemon juice, cinnamon and ground ginger and place in the baking dish.

3 Mix together all the crumble ingredients in a mixing bowl or food processor until you have a crumbly texture.

4 Sprinkle the crumble topping over the fruit and bake in the preheated oven for 35–40 minutes or until the crumble is golden brown.

Serving suggestions Serve with plain Greek yoghurt or ice cream.

Hints and variations For a more formal meal, you could bake the crumble in individual ramekins, reducing the cooking time slightly. Clean any burned crumbs or splashes of fruit from around the sides of the dishes before serving.

NATURALLY BALANCED Muscovado sugar is as calorie-laden as any other sugar but, since it is one of the least refined of sugars, it does retain much of its nutritional goodness. This is reflected in its deep, rich taste. Because of its strong flavour, you do not need to use very much.

49

FOOD FOR THE FAMILY

Baked custard tart with bay leaves

Herbs and spices have always been used to add subtle flavouring to baked custards. Vanilla pods and nutmeg are amongst the most common but in this case I have also used bay leaves, another traditional favourite.

MAKES 4–6 PORTIONS

FOR THE PASTRY (PASTE)
175 g/6 oz/1½ cups unbleached plain (all-purpose) flour

100 g/4 oz/½ cup salted butter, softened

15 ml/1 tbsp unrefined caster (superfine) sugar

A pinch of sea salt

1 large free-range egg, beaten

1 free-range egg yolk, for brushing

FOR THE CUSTARD
3 large free-range eggs

65 g/2½ oz/⅓ cup unrefined caster sugar

A few drops of vanilla essence (extract)

400 ml/14 fl oz/1¾ cups full-fat milk

3 bay leaves

A pinch of freshly grated nutmeg (optional)

1 Preheat the oven to 180°C/350°F/gas 4/fan oven 160°C. Grease a 20 cm/8 in flan tin (pie pan) and place it on a baking (cookie) tray.

2 To make the pastry, place the flour, butter, sugar and salt in a food processor and blend very briefly to mix. Add the egg and blend for 5–10 seconds until just holding together. If necessary, add a little cold water and blend again for another 5 seconds. Do not be tempted to process the pastry too long, otherwise it will become tough.

3 Roll out the pastry thinly on a lightly floured surface and leave to rest for 10–15 minutes.

4 Line the prepared tin with the pastry, cover with baking parchment and add a handful of baking beans. Bake blind in the preheated oven for 15–18 minutes. Remove from the oven and remove the paper and beans. Brush the pastry with the beaten egg yolk, then return to the oven for a further 3–4 minutes.

5 While the base is baking, make the egg custard mix. Beat the eggs, sugar and vanilla essence together with a wooden spoon, then add the milk. Do not over-beat the mixture and make it frothy, otherwise it will not remain level while cooking.

6 Pour the custard into the cooked pastry case (pie shell), add the bay leaves and sprinkle generously with grated nutmeg, if liked. Bake in the preheated oven for 40–50 minutes or until a definite skin has formed on top and the centre feels firm to the touch. Remove from the oven and leave to cool before serving.

Serving suggestions This baked custard tart is delicious on its own, but it does also marry nicely with Lime-marinated Strawberries (see page 132) or perhaps Whisky and Honey Ice Cream (see page 133).

Hints and variations Resting the rolled-out pastry produces a better lining, less likely to shrink when baked. I always brush the baked pastry with egg yolk, then bake for a few minutes longer in the oven before filling, to form a seal between the custard and the pastry. This helps keep the base crisp for this custard tart.

NATURALLY BALANCED In general, we should avoid using a lot of sugar in our diet, especially white sugar as it consists of completely empty calories, stripped of all nutrients. When you do use sugar, it makes good sense to switch to unrefined varieties, as these have not been bleached and retain many nutrients.

food for FUN

Although preparing meals day in, day out may sometimes be a chore, cooking can also be great fun and is a really fascinating process. The kitchen is like a laboratory where you can discover by experimentation what works – and what doesn't! Children love the exploratory nature of cooking and the completeness of the process – starting off with the basic ingredients and eventually producing something scrumptious to eat, so do bring younger members of the family into the kitchen to help you. Be rigid about hygiene and safety, but allow them the freedom to explore the infinite ways in which ingredients can be combined to form interesting and delicious dishes. Encourage children to use all five senses: sight, touch, smell, hearing and last, but not least, taste!

Melting mozzarella toasts

This is an Italian version of cheese on toast, although it is rather lighter and not as high in saturated fats as its traditional counterpart. These little toasts are easy enough for the kids to master and perhaps eat as part of their meal, or you could even use this recipe as the starter of an impressive dinner party.

MAKES 8 SMALL TOASTS

1 ciabatta loaf, cut into 8 thin slices

30 ml/2 tbsp cold-pressed virgin olive oil

1 garlic clove, halved and skin left on

100 g/4 oz Mozzarella cheese, cut into 8 thin slices

Sea salt and freshly ground black pepper

30 ml/2 tbsp chopped fresh parsley

Juice of ½ small lemon

1 Preheat the oven to 200°C/400°F/gas 6/fan oven 180°C.

2 Lay the ciabatta slices on a baking (cookie) tray and brush with half the olive oil.

3 Bake in the preheated oven for 12–14 minutes until they look and feel like toast.

4 Remove from the oven and rub each toast with the cut sides of the garlic clove. Don't press the garlic too hard on the toast or the flavour will be too strong.

5 Lay a slice of Mozzarella on each toast and sprinkle with a little salt and pepper. Return the baking tray to the oven for a further couple of minutes until the cheese has melted.

6 Meanwhile, chop the parsley and mix with the remaining olive oil and the lemon juice.

7 Transfer the toasts to warm plates and drizzle with the olive oil and lemon dressing.

Serving suggestions These make a simple starter with a few green leaves. Alternatively, serve as a light main course with my Tomato and Chilli Salad (see page 27).

NATURALLY BALANCED Virgin olive oil is an excellent source of oleic acid, which helps contribute nourishment to many parts of the body, such as the hair and nails. Olive oil is a poor source of the essential fatty acids omega-3 and omega-6, however – but they are found in abundance in seeds and oily fish, which emphasises the need for a naturally balanced diet containing a wide range of nutritious foods.

Home-made burger buns

This recipe is an ideal way for the kids to experiment with making bread.
They can make these soft rolls as large or as small as they like, to hold their
home-made burgers.
   See photograph opposite page 49.

MAKES 8–10 LARGE ROLLS

500 g/18 oz/4½ cups strong plain (bread) flour

200 g/7 oz/1¾ cups wholemeal plain (all-purpose) flour

1 sachet of easy-blend dried yeast

2.5 ml/½ tsp sea salt

5 ml/1 tsp unrefined caster (superfine) sugar

200 ml/7 fl oz/scant 1 cup lukewarm milk, plus a little extra for brushing

250 ml/8 fl oz/1 cup lukewarm water

25 g/1 oz/¼ cup sesame or poppy seeds

1 Preheat the oven to 220°C/425°F/gas 7/fan oven 200°C.

2 Mix together the flours, yeast, salt and sugar. Add the milk and water and mix in with your fingers to form a dough. Turn on to a floured surface and knead for 5 minutes until the dough is soft and elastic.

3 Put the dough back into the bowl and cover with a damp tea towel (dish cloth). Leave to stand in a warm place for about 1 hour until doubled in size.

4 Knead the dough again lightly to knock out the air; this is called knocking back (punching down).

5 Divide the dough into about 10 portions, shape each one into a round ball, then flatten out a little. Place on greased baking (cookie) trays, leaving enough room for them to rise. Cover again and leave to rise for about 30 minutes until doubled in size.

6 Press your thumb into the centre of each roll, which will make the surface slightly flat rather than domed. Brush with a little milk and scatter over the seeds.

7 Bake in the preheated oven for about 10 minutes until golden and hollow-sounding when tapped on the base.

8 Transfer to a wire cooling rack, cover with a dry tea towel and leave to cool. This will help to keep them soft rather than crusty.

Serving suggestions Of course, these are ideal for burgers (see page 55 for my giant ones), but they are also perfect for filling for lunch boxes or for serving with meals.

NATURALLY BALANCED *The wholemeal flour adds a wonderful taste and texture to the rolls and also provides essential fibre.*

Giant burgers

Buying take-away food is a treat, but home-made burgers are so much better in terms of texture, smell and, above all, taste. And you'll know exactly what goes into them!
See photograph opposite page 49.

MAKES 2 GIANT BURGERS

15 ml/1 tbsp sunflower oil

½ onion, finely chopped

30 ml/2 tbsp dried breadcrumbs

15 ml/1 tbsp tomato ketchup (catsup)

200 g/7 oz lean minced (ground) beef

1 small free-range egg, beaten

**Sea salt and
freshly ground black pepper**

1 Heat a non-stick frying pan (skillet), add the oil and heat gently. Add the onion and sauté for about 2 minutes until transparent.

2 Remove the pan from the heat and mix in the breadcrumbs and tomato ketchup. Allow to cool slightly.

3 Break up the minced beef with a fork in a bowl. Add the sautéed onion mixture and beaten egg, and season with salt and pepper. Mix all the ingredients together well, squeezing with your hands. If the mixture feels very wet at this stage, add a few more breadcrumbs. Divide and shape the mixture into two giant burgers (or four small ones, if preferred).

4 Preheat the grill (broiler) to maximum.

5 Cook the burgers under the hot grill for about 8 minutes each side, depending on thickness, until they are cooked through and browned.

Serving suggestions These go perfectly with my Home-made Burger Buns (see page 54), which can be made to size, of course! Slice the buns in half and insert the burgers, adding sliced gherkins, American mustard and tomato ketchup – or whatever takes your fancy. Garnish with a crisp green salad for a nutritionally balanced meal.

Hints and variations Do remember to wash your hands before and after handling raw meat.

NATURALLY BALANCED A beefburger can make a nutritious meal as long as it is made from top-quality ingredients. This doesn't apply to cheap commercially made burgers, which are usually filled out with bulking agents and hydrogenated fats to help preserve their shelf life.

Home-made oven-baked chips

Home-made chips (fries) do take a little effort, but if you can spare the time then these oven-baked chips are a winner, extremely low in fat and rich in vitamin C. The only problem is that once you've eaten one, you'll find it hard to stop!
See photograph opposite page 49.

MAKES 4–6 PORTIONS

A little sunflower oil

8–10 Maris Piper or King Edward potatoes

Sea salt

Malt vinegar (optional)

1 Preheat the oven to 200°C/400°F/gas 6/fan oven 180°C and brush a large roasting tin (pan) with sunflower oil.

2 Bring a large pan of salted water to the boil. Meanwhile, peel and wash the potatoes and cut into fingers about 1 cm/½ in thick. Add to the boiling water and cook for 4 minutes.

3 Drain immediately, then return the chips to the dry pan. Cover with a tight-fitting lid and shake the pan to start releasing the starch. This helps create a crisp coating when the chips are baked.

4 Tip the chunky chips into the prepared roasting tin, spread them out and brush each with a little more oil.

5 Bake in the preheated oven for 25–30 minutes, turning a few times during cooking, until the chips are crisp and golden brown.

6 Remove from the oven and place on kitchen paper (paper towels) to drain before transferring to a warm serving dish and seasoning with a little salt and vinegar, if liked.

Serving suggestions The perfect accompaniment to my Giant Burgers (see page 55), these chips will go well with just about anything!

Hints and variations The chips will stay crisp once made. If you want to prepare and cook them in advance, they can be flashed back in a hot oven for 5–6 minutes to reheat when you are ready to serve.

NATURALLY BALANCED Potatoes are a good source of the mineral potassium, which is recommended for anyone who eats a diet rich in salt and sugar.

FOOD FOR FUN

Goats' cheese and tomato baguette slices

Easy to master and simply delicious, serve these as part of the kids' dinner. Better still, let the kids loose in the kitchen and just keep an eye on them while they make the slices for themselves!

MAKES 4 SLICES

1 baguette

30 ml/2 tbsp cold-pressed virgin olive oil

5 ml/1 tsp dried rosemary

150 g/5 oz/generous 1 cup soft goats' cheese

30 ml/2 tbsp crème fraîche

Sea salt and freshly ground black pepper

15 ml/1 tbsp tomato purée (paste)

1 Preheat the oven to 200°C/400°F/gas 6/fan oven 180°C.

2 Cut the baguette in half lengthways, then in half horizontally to make four pieces. Place the slices on a baking (cookie) tray, drizzle with the oil and sprinkle over the rosemary.

3 Bake in the preheated oven for 10–12 minutes until golden brown.

4 Meanwhile, use a fork to mix together the goats' cheese and crème fraîche in a bowl, then season with a little salt and pepper.

5 Once the toasts are ready, spread tomato purée on each slice, then top with the goats' cheese mixture. Place them back in the oven for a further 4 minutes until hot and melting.

Serving suggestions These go well with Home-made Oven-baked Chips (see page 56) for a really natural-style pizza and chips (fries). You can also serve the toasts as a cold lunch dish, if there are any left – but somehow I doubt there will be.

NATURALLY BALANCED Many people, including a large proportion of youngsters, have trouble digesting cows' milk. Although sheep's and goats' milk are similar to cows', they both contain less fat. Also the fat globules in goats' milk are far easier for the body to break down and digest.

Banana and oat scotch pancakes

These pancakes are a really simple but tasty, wholesome dessert for young children or teenagers to make.

MAKES ABOUT 12 PANCAKES

50 g/2 oz/¼ cup salted butter, softened

225 g/8 oz/2 cups unbleached self-raising (self-rising) flour

100 g/4 oz/1 cup rolled porridge oats

50 g/2 oz/¼ cup unrefined caster (superfine) sugar

1 large free-range egg, beaten

175 ml/6 fl oz/¾ cup milk

A pinch of sea salt

A pinch of ground cinnamon

4 large ripe bananas

100 ml/3½ fl oz/scant ½ cup plain set Greek yoghurt

30 ml/2 tbsp maple syrup

1 Rub half the butter into the flour, then stir in the oats and sugar. Add the beaten egg, then gradually stir in the milk and season with salt and cinnamon.

2 Peel and mash two of the bananas, then beat them into the mixture.

3 Heat a heavy-based frying pan (skillet) on a medium to high heat and lightly grease with a little of the remaining butter. Drop spoonfuls of the mixture into the pan and cook for about 3 minutes on each side. Remove them from the pan once they are cooked and keep them warm while you cook the remaining pancakes in the same way.

4 Slice the remaining bananas and arrange a few slices on top of each pancake. Spoon a little Greek yoghurt on top, then drizzle with maple syrup.

Hints and variations The pancakes freeze well, without the banana slices and yoghurt. Make them in advance, in bulk, if you prefer, then layer them with greaseproof (waxed) paper, wrap and freeze. You can then take them out individually when required. Defrost in the microwave for 1–2 minutes per pancake, then eat for breakfast or use as part of a lunch box.

NATURALLY BALANCED Bananas have long been known as an excellent source of potassium. This mineral is helpful for maintaining blood sugar levels and is essential to restore a correct balance for anyone who eats a lot of salted, processed food.

Apple and apricot treacle tart bars

These are fun to make and taste gorgeous. The combination of apple and apricot really helps to make the tart something special and the sweet flavour of the fruit means that you only need a small amount of golden syrup.

MAKES ABOUT 12 BARS

100 g/4 oz/½ cup unsalted (sweet) butter, softened

50 g/2 oz/¼ cup muscovado sugar

175 g/6 oz/1½ cups unbleached plain (all-purpose) flour

450 g/1 lb eating (dessert) apples, peeled and cored

175 g/6 oz/1 cup ready-to-eat dried unsulphured apricots

Grated zest and juice of ½ lemon

50 g/2 oz/½ cup rolled porridge oats

Grated zest and juice of 1 orange

175 g/6 oz/½ cup golden (light corn) syrup

1 Preheat the oven to 190°C/375°F/gas 5/fan oven 170°C and grease a 20 cm/8 in square baking tin (pan) with a ridged base.

2 Beat together the butter and muscovado sugar until light and fluffy, then mix in the flour until all the ingredients are well blended.

3 Spread the mixture in the base of the prepared tin, press down lightly until flat, then lightly prick with a fork. Bake in the preheated oven for 10–12 minutes until golden.

4 While the base is cooking, chop the apples and apricots in a food processor, then add the lemon zest and juice and half the oats and blend to a fine purée.

5 Mix the orange zest and juice with the syrup and the remaining oats.

6 Remove the base from the oven and pour in the apple and apricot filling, then spread with the orange topping, covering the filling completely to prevent the sides from burning.

7 Return to the oven for 20–25 minutes until set and pale golden.

8 Remove from the oven, score lightly on top into 12 bars, then leave to cool completely in the tray – overnight if possible – before cutting.

Serving suggestions These bars make ideal lunch-box snacks. They are also delicious warmed in the oven for 4–5 minutes and served with plain yoghurt or ice cream.

Hints and variations The bars freeze well for up to three months.

NATURALLY BALANCED Oats are a good source of soluble fibre, and slow down the absorption of carbohydrates, so helpng to keep blood sugar levels balanced.

Foolproof chocolate cake with fudge coating

This is a perfectly divine recipe, which has been passed down through generations of my family. Adding hot water to activate the baking powder makes the cake especially light and the rich chocolate fudge topping is wonderfully wicked.

MAKES 6 PORTIONS

100 g/4 oz/½ cup unsalted (sweet) butter or unhydrogenated margarine, softened

200 g/7 oz/scant 1 cup unrefined caster (superfine) sugar

2 large free-range eggs, beaten

30 ml/2 tbsp cocoa (unsweetened chocolate) powder

175 g/6 oz/1½ cups unbleached self-raising (self-rising) flour

45 ml/3 tbsp warm milk

5 ml/1 tsp baking powder

45 ml/3 tbsp warm water

FOR THE FUDGE TOPPING

50 g/2 oz/¼ cup salted butter or unhydrogenated margarine

15 ml/1 tbsp milk

60 ml/4 tbsp icing (confectioners') sugar, sifted

15 ml/1 tbsp cocoa powder

1 Preheat the oven to 160°C/325°F/gas 3/fan oven 145°C and grease a 15 cm/6 in cake tin (pan).

2 Cream together the butter or margarine and sugar until light and fluffy, beat in the eggs and cocoa powder, then fold in the flour and stir in the milk.

3 Add the baking powder to the warm water, then stir it into the mixture.

4 Pour into the prepared tin and bake in the preheated oven for 35–45 minutes until firm to the touch. Turn out on to a wire rack to cool.

5 To make the fudge topping, gently melt the butter or margarine in a pan, then mix in the milk, followed by the icing sugar and cocoa. Remove from the heat and stir well until you have a smooth and creamy, but not runny, fudge topping. If the mixture is too runny, blend in a little more icing sugar.

6 When the cake is completely cold, spread with the fudge icing and serve.

Serving suggestions The cake is delicious just as it is, but if you're feeling really indulgent, split the cooled cake and fill with whipped double (heavy) cream and fresh soft fruit before topping with the fudge icing. Choose whatever fruit you like best for the filling; my own favourite is raspberries!

NATURALLY BALANCED Many commercially made cakes are made with hydrogenated or trans-fatty acids. These are believed to be chemically unstable and detrimental to the body and should ideally be avoided, both in baked goods and soft margarines.

Dairy-free chocolate and orange cake

For those who have an intolerance to dairy products – and this affects many adults and children – it can be difficult to find dairy-free cakes, and the minefield of ingredients on food does not make things any easier. This recipe is perfect for anyone who loves chocolate but needs to avoid dairy products.

MAKES 6–8 PORTIONS

300 g/11 oz/2¾ cups unbleached self-raising (self-rising) flour

15 ml/1 tbsp baking powder

50 g/2 oz/½ cup cocoa (unsweetened chocolate) powder

250 g/9 oz/generous 1 cup unrefined caster (superfine) sugar

5 ml/1 tsp vanilla essence (extract)

300 ml/½ pt/1¼ cups orange juice

200 ml/7 fl oz/scant 1 cup sunflower oil

30 ml/2 tbsp orange flower water

1 Preheat the oven to 180°C/350°F/gas 4/fan oven 160°C and grease a 900 g/2 lb loaf tin (pan) or deep 18 cm/7 in cake tin.

2 Sift the flour, baking powder and cocoa into a large mixing bowl, then add the sugar and vanilla essence.

3 Mix together the orange juice, sunflower oil and orange flower water, then pour into the dry ingredients, stirring all the time until the ingredients have blended into a batter consistency. Pour into the prepared tin.

4 Bake in the preheated oven for about 40 minutes or until set in the centre.

5 Turn out on to a wire rack to cool completely.

Serving suggestions You can simply serve the cake on its own, or you can cover it with Fudge Coating (use the recipe on page 60 but replace the milk with soya milk).

NATURALLY BALANCED There are many symptoms of an intolerance to dairy products, sinus problems or bloating and diarrhoea being among the most common. If you are experiencing such symptoms, you should always consult your doctor. Many people nowadays choose to avoid dairy products because of the use of the chemical lindane in the processing of milk, as there have been suggestions that this may have a negative health effect.

Fruited flapjacks with pumpkin and sunflower seeds

*If you have children in your family – or adults for that matter – who could do with
a little less sugar in their diet but love sweet things, then try making these
delicious snacks.*

MAKES 8 PORTIONS

150 g/5 oz/⅔ cup unsalted (sweet)
butter or unhydrogenated margarine

180 ml/6 fl oz/¾ cup apple concentrate

225 g/8 oz/2 cups rolled porridge oats

100 g/4 oz/⅔ cup sultanas
(golden raisins)

25 g/1 oz/¼ cup pumpkin seeds

25 g/1 oz/¼ cup sunflower seeds

A pinch of sea salt

1 Preheat the oven to 190°C/375°F/gas 5/fan oven 170°C. Generously grease a 20 cm/8 in square cake tin (pan).

2 Gently melt the butter or margarine with the apple concentrate in a saucepan.

3 Stir in the oats, sultanas, seeds and salt.

4 Spoon the mixture into the prepared tin, press down and smooth the top level.

5 Bake in the preheated oven for 20–25 minutes until golden brown.

6 Remove from the oven and mark into eight pieces, then leave to cool in the tin. When completely cool, remove from the tin and cut into bars.

Hints and variations These flapjacks store well in a sealed airtight container. They can also be frozen.

Apple concentrate is widely available in health food shops. Don't try to use apple purée or concentrated juice – they definitely won't work!

NATURALLY BALANCED Pumpkin and sunflower seeds contain large quantities of the essential fatty acids omega-3 and omega-6.

Ginger and honey tuille biscuits

These biscuits (cookies) are very simple to make and they are great fun to shape into domes, baskets, curves, or anything else you fancy.

MAKES 12–14 BISCUITS

100 g/4 oz/½ cup salted butter

200 g/7 oz/scant 1 cup unrefined caster (superfine) sugar

75 ml/5 tbsp clear honey

2.5 ml/½ tsp ground ginger

175 g/6 oz/1½ cups unbleached plain (all-purpose) flour

4 large free-range egg whites

1 Preheat the oven to 200°C/400°F/gas 6/fan oven 180°C and line a baking (cookie) tray with a non-stick baking mat or baking parchment.

2 Melt the butter in a saucepan, then mix in the sugar, honey and ginger until well blended.

3 Add the flour and egg whites, beating all the time, until the mixture is smooth and pliable.

4 Place teaspoonfuls of the mixture on to the baking mat or parchment and spread out, using a circular movement. (A little tip: use a few tiny blobs of the tuille mixture to secure the mat or parchment to the tray – it stops it sliding about.) Leave plenty of room between the tuilles as the mixture will spread.

5 Bake in the preheated oven for 12–14 minutes until golden brown.

6 To shape the biscuits, find some kitchen objects to use as moulds – an upturned ramekin (custard cup) or coffee cup for example. When you remove the tray from the oven, gently lift the biscuits immediately on to their moulds and curve them to your desired shape. Leave to cool and set. Alternatively, lift the flat biscuits on to a wire rack and leave them to cool completely.

Serving suggestions Try making little baskets and filling them with my Lime-marinated Strawberries (see page 132), or my Lemon and Lime Curd (see page 130).

Hints and variations Stored in an airtight container, the biscuits will stay beautifully crisp for two or three days.

NATURALLY BALANCED Honey contains more minerals and enzymes than sugar and therefore does not upset the body's mineral balance as much as sugar does.

Butter shortbread hearts

Simple, delicious and perfect for children to make to show their parents how much they love them – or vice versa, of course! For perfect heart-shaped biscuits (cookies), you will need a special cutter, but you can make any shape you like.

MAKES ABOUT 8 SMALL HEARTS

75 g/3 oz/⅓ cup salted butter, softened

25 g/1 oz/2 tbsp unrefined caster (superfine) sugar, plus extra for sprinkling

75 g/3 oz/¾ cup unbleached plain (all-purpose) flour

25 g/1 oz/3 tbsp fine semolina or ground almonds

1 Preheat the oven to 150°C/300°F/gas 2/fan oven 135°C and grease an 18 cm/7 in cake tin (pan).

2 Cream together the butter and sugar in a bowl, then work in the flour and semolina or almonds and use your fingertips to knead until smooth.

3 Press into the prepared tin and flatten with a palette knife. The mixture should be about 5 mm/¼ in thick. Prick all over with a fork.

4 Bake in the preheated oven for 30–35 minutes until lightly golden.

5 Remove from the oven and while the shortbread is still warm, cut out your shapes with the cutter, keeping them as close together as possible. Sprinkle with a little sugar, then transfer to a wire rack to cool. Treat yourself by finishing off the in-between bits!

NATURALLY BALANCED Make sure you put plenty of love into the preparation of these little hearts – then, hopefully, they will bring love to all those who eat them!

Wheat-free peanut butter cookies

Many people have an intolerance to gluten, the protein found in wheat, which may cause anything from a vague sense of feeling off-colour to a serious allergic reaction. This recipe makes delicious peanut butter cookies to be enjoyed whether you are avoiding wheat or not.

MAKES ABOUT 8 COOKIES

175 g/6 oz/¾ cup soft brown sugar

125 g/4½ oz/generous ½ cup unsalted (sweet) butter

125 g/4½ oz/generous ½ cup organic crunchy peanut butter

1 large free-range egg, beaten

175 g/6 oz/1½ cups rice flour

5 ml/1 tsp baking powder

5 ml/1 tsp vanilla essence (extract)

1 Preheat the oven to 180°C/350°F/gas 4/fan oven 160°C and grease a baking (cookie) tray.

2 Cream together the sugar and butter until light and fluffy.

3 Beat in the peanut butter and egg, followed by the flour, baking powder and vanilla essence until you have a soft dough.

4 Using a dessertspoon, place mounds of cookie dough on the prepared baking tray, evenly spaced apart.

5 Bake in the preheated oven for 16–18 minutes until just golden brown. Don't overcook them – they are best served just slightly under-done.

6 Remove from the oven and leave on a wire rack to cool completely.

Hints and variations It's fun to make these as giant saucer-sized cookies– just cook them for a further 5–7 minutes. The cookies will keep in an airtight container for two or three days and they also freeze well.

NATURALLY BALANCED Some people believe the problem with gluten is linked to the overuse of the refined cheap flour that is often used to make processed wheat products, as extra gluten powder or flour improver is often added to products such as white bread, to make them lighter. An excess of gluten in the diet, or a gluten intolerance, is often directly linked to bowel and digestion disorders.

food for FRIENDS

Throughout history, preparing and serving food for others has been an enduring sign of peace and fellowship. It doesn't cost much but it says such a lot.

Be sure to keep it simple. The meal should not detract from the conversation at the table or be so complex that you have to be away for long periods or get into a flap.

Presentation makes a big difference when you are entertaining. Fresh flowers, a jug of water and warm bread give a feeling of warmth and closeness.

To finish the meal, try serving a herbal infusion, such as lemon and ginger. They make a change from coffee or tea and will be welcomed by the increasing number of people who find that caffeine at night keeps them awake.

Mushroom fricassee on toast with cranberry

I have always found the flavours of mushrooms and cranberries make an excellent combination and this dish is a classic example of how they harmonise together. Serve this delicious dish on little slices of crunchy toast as an easy and elegant starter, or use the fricassee for a special main course supper dish.

MAKES 4 PORTIONS AS A STARTER OR 2 AS A MAIN COURSE

½ medium baguette

25 g/1 oz/2 tbsp unsalted (sweet) butter, melted

Sea salt and freshly ground black pepper

25 g/1 oz/2 tbsp salted butter

4 shallots or 1 large onion, chopped

2 garlic cloves, crushed

5 ml/1 tsp dried sage

600 g/1 lb 6 oz button mushrooms, halved

200 ml/7 fl oz/scant 1 cup white wine

10 ml/2 tsp cornflour (cornstarch)

100 ml/3½ fl oz/scant ½ cup vegetable stock

30 ml/2 tbsp crème fraîche or soured (dairy sour) cream

15 ml/1 tbsp cranberry sauce

15 ml/1 tbsp chopped fresh tarragon or parsley

1 Preheat the oven to 200°C/400°F/gas 6/fan oven 180°C.

2 Cut the baguette into eight slices and place on a baking (cookie) tray, brush with the melted unsalted butter and sprinkle with a little salt and pepper. Bake in the preheated oven for 10–12 minutes until golden.

3 Meanwhile, heat a large frying pan (skillet) or sauté pan and melt the salted butter. Add the shallots or onion, the garlic and sage and sauté for 1 minute.

4 Add the mushrooms and continue to sauté for a further 2 minutes until they are thoroughly coated in the butter and sage. Add the white wine and boil for a couple of minutes to reduce slightly.

5 Thoroughly whisk the cornflour into the vegetable stock, then add the mixture to the mushrooms.

6 Reserve a spoonful each of the crème fraîche and cranberry sauce for garnish, then stir the remainder into the pan. Bring to the boil, reduce the heat, then simmer for 5 minutes.

7 Remove the toasts from the oven and arrange on individual plates.

8 Stir the tarragon or parsley into the mushrooms, then spoon over the toasts and garnish with a little crème fraîche and cranberry sauce.

Serving suggestions For a starter, I would simply serve the fricassee with some warm bread and a few salad leaves. For an impressive main course, make Crispy Filo Baskets (see page 135) and serve the fricassee tumbling out of them.

NATURALLY BALANCED It is well documented that many types of mushroom have healing properties and research into mushrooms is continually making new discoveries. Even the common button mushroom has been found to help cut the fat level in the blood.

Mixed vegetable pakoras

Pakoras make a perfect appetiser for your friends to tuck into before a main meal, or a delicious and very sociable snack. They are created from a selection of vegetables dipped in a spiced Indian batter and are cooked in fresh, hot groundnut or sunflower oil so that they are light and crisp and not at all greasy.

MAKES 20–25 SMALL FRITTERS (ABOUT 4 PORTIONS)

FOR THE BATTER

225 g/8 oz/2 cups gram flour

5 ml/1 tsp chilli powder

5 ml/1 tsp ground fenugreek

1.5 ml/¼ tsp ground cinnamon

1.5 ml/¼ tsp ground ginger

1.5 ml/¼ tsp ground turmeric

1.5 ml/¼ tsp garlic powder

Sea salt

20 ml/1½ tbsp lemon juice

300 ml/½ pt/1¼ cups water

Groundnut (peanut) or sunflower oil, for deep-frying

1 aubergine (eggplant), thinly sliced

1 small cauliflower, cut into small florets

8 button mushrooms

8 baby sweetcorn (corn), cut in half

1 Put the gram flour with all the spices and 5 ml/1 tsp sea salt in a bowl. Stir to mix, then gradually whisk in the lemon juice and enough of the water to form a slightly runny paste. Leave to stand for 5 minutes while you prepare the vegetables.

2 Heat the groundnut or sunflower oil in a deep-fat fryer or wok to 190°C/375°F, when a cube of day-old bread will brown in 30 seconds. Preheat the oven to 120°C/250°F/gas ½/fan oven 110°C.

3 Add the prepared vegetables to the batter, making sure they are all thoroughly coated.

4 Use a fork or tongs to lift the vegetables out of the batter in small batches and lower gently into the hot oil. They will cook in just a few minutes and rise to the surface, crisp and golden brown. Remove from the oil with a draining spoon, drain on kitchen paper (paper towels), then arrange on an ovenproof serving plate and keep hot in the preheated oven while you cook the remaining pakoras.

5 Sprinkle with a pinch of sea salt before serving.

Serving suggestions These vegetable pakoras are delicious served with mango chutney. Alternatively, garnish them with wedges of lemon and fresh sprigs of coriander (cilantro) and serve with some plain set yoghurt on the side.

Hints and variations To make life even easier, you can precook the pakoras, then dip a few at a time into hot oil to reheat just as your guests arrive.

NATURALLY BALANCED Groundnut oil is now readily available in both supermarkets and health food shops. It is a great choice for cooking as it oxidises at a much higher temperature than other oils, especially blended vegetable oil.

Cashew and quinoa cheese loaf

Unfortunately, nut loaf still suffers from the stigma of cranky 1970s vegetarianism – but don't make that mistake and miss out on this delicious twenty-first-century version! Believe me, the nut loaf has come a long way. The deep taste and texture combined with a rich sauce make this one a feast in its own right.

MAKES 6 PORTIONS

30 ml/2 tbsp sunflower oil

2 onions, finely diced

5 ml/1 tsp medium curry powder

4 celery sticks, finely chopped

250 g/9 oz/2¼ cups quinoa grain

15 ml/1 tbsp tomato purée (paste)

5 ml/1 tsp dried sage

750 ml/1¼ pts/3 cups vegetable stock

250 g/9 oz/2¼ cups roasted and salted cashew nuts

250 g/9 oz/2¼ cups Cheddar or red Leicester cheese, grated

3 large free-range eggs, beaten

5 ml/1 tsp paprika

150 g/5 oz/1¼ cups dried breadcrumbs

Sea salt and freshly ground black pepper

1 Preheat the oven to 190°C/375°F/gas 5/fan oven 170°C. Grease and line a 900 g/2 lb loaf tin (pan).

2 Heat the sunflower oil in a large saucepan, add the onions and sauté for 1–2 minutes until beginning to soften.

3 Add the curry powder and celery and sauté for a further 2 minutes, stirring well, until the ingredients have softened and absorbed the curry powder.

4 Stir in the quinoa, tomato purée and dried sage, then add the stock and bring to the boil. Reduce the heat and simmer, uncovered, for 14 minutes or until the stock has all been absorbed, stirring occasionally.

5 Meanwhile, crush the cashew nuts in a bag or cloth until they are coarsely broken up. Mix the nuts with the cheese, eggs and paprika.

6 Stir the breadcrumbs into the pan, then mix in the nut and cheese mixture and season to taste with a little salt and pepper.

7 Spoon the mixture into the prepared loaf tin and pat down firmly, then cover with greaseproof (waxed) paper. Bake in the preheated oven for about 45 minutes or until firm in the middle to the touch.

Serving suggestions Serve slices of the loaf on a bed of mashed potatoes with perhaps a few seasonal vegetables. Caramelised Onion Sauce (see page 124) makes the ideal accompaniment.

NATURALLY BALANCED Since quinoa is gluten-free, this recipe is ideal for anyone who is avoiding gluten in their diet – but you must also use gluten-free breadcrumbs, which you can buy easily in health food shops.

Alsace caramelised onion tart

This uses a bread dough base like a pizza. I have adapted the recipe from its classic roots in Alsace on the French–German border. The onions are lightly caramelised to sweeten their taste before being spread over the bread base and the crunchy cheese crumble topping gives the tart its wonderful texture.

**MAKES 6 PORTIONS AS A STARTER OR
4 PORTIONS AS A MAIN COURSE**

FOR THE BREAD BASE
150 g/5 oz/1¼ cups wholemeal plain
(all-purpose) flour

150 g/5 oz/1¼ cups unbleached plain
(all-purpose) flour

15 ml/1 tbsp muscovado sugar

1 sachet of easy-blend dried yeast

5 ml/1 tsp sea salt

100 ml/3½ fl oz/scant ½ cup warm water

60 ml/4 tbsp sunflower oil

FOR THE ONION TOPPING
15 ml/1 tbsp sunflower oil, for cooking

4 onions, thinly sliced

25 g/1 oz/2 tbsp muscovado sugar

5 ml/1 tsp dried mixed herbs

50 g/2 oz/¼ cup salted butter

100 g/4 oz/1 cup Cheddar cheese,
grated or crumbled

100 g/4 oz/1 cup dried breadcrumbs

30 ml/2 tbsp chopped fresh parsley

Sea salt and
freshly ground black pepper

1 Preheat the oven to 220ºC/425ºF/gas 7/fan oven 200ºC and grease a large baking (cookie) tray.

2 In a large mixing bowl, mix together the flours, sugar, yeast and salt, then add the water and oil and mix to a soft but firm dough. Knead for a couple of minutes until pliable and no longer sticky. You can do this in a mixer with a dough hook or in your food processor if you prefer.

3 Using a rolling pin, roll the dough flat on a lightly floured surface to about 1 cm/½ in thick. Lay the dough on the prepared baking tray and press out towards the edges.

4 To make the onion topping, heat a large frying pan (skillet), add the oil and place over a high heat for a few seconds. Add the onions, sugar and mixed herbs, then turn down the heat to medium, add the butter and leave to caramelise slowly, stirring occasionally to prevent the onions catching. Cook for about 5–6 minutes until the onions have softened and darkened slightly.

5 Meanwhile, mix together the cheese, breadcrumbs and parsley to form a soft, crumble-like consistency.

6 When the onions are ready, season with salt and pepper, then spread on to the dough base. Sprinkle the cheese crumble topping liberally over the onions in an even layer.

7 Bake in the preheated oven for 20–25 minutes until the crumble has turned golden brown.

Serving suggestions This onion tart goes perfectly with my Sauté of Spinach and Garlic (see page 86), with a dollop of Sweet Tomato Dressing (see page 128) as a sauce. The tart is also delicious served cold, so it makes a perfect lunch-box dish.

Hints and variations You can use any cheese you like, or even use up leftovers.

NATURALLY BALANCED Onions contain many important nutrients. The two most beneficial are the compounds called allicin and sulforaphane, both of which are believed to reduce the risk of certain cancers. I like to use refined sunflower oil when it is available as it is the best quality.

Baked butternut squash with rosemary and walnut gratin

Butternut squash are readily available in supermarkets and greengrocers. They have a tough outer skin that protects the velvety yellow flesh inside.

MAKES 4 PORTIONS

1 butternut squash, about 600 g/1 lb 6 oz

5 ml/1 tsp dried rosemary

Sea salt and freshly ground black pepper

100 ml/3½ fl oz/scant ½ cup cold-pressed virgin olive oil

100 g/4 oz/1 cup walnut pieces

3 slices of wholemeal bread, cut into small chunks

100 g/4 oz/1 cup hard cheese such as Cheddar or red Leicester, coarsely grated

15 ml/1 tbsp chopped fresh parsley

1 Preheat the oven to 220°C/425°F/gas 7/fan oven 200°C.

2 Cut the squash in half, then into quarters. Remove the seeds and then score the flesh in a 'criss-cross' pattern with a small knife. Place on a large ovenproof dish, season with rosemary, salt and pepper and drizzle with the olive oil.

3 Bake in the preheated oven for 40–45 minutes until soft in the centre.

4 Meanwhile, break the walnuts into small pieces with your fingers, then mix with the bread, cheese and parsley.

5 Remove the squash from the oven and sprinkle with the cheese topping. Return to the oven for 12 minutes until the cheese has melted and the surface is crisp and golden. Serve hot.

Serving suggestions Sauté of Spinach and Garlic (see page 86) makes a nice light accompaniment to this recipe. Lay the baked squash on a bed of the spinach and serve with Citrus and Ginger Dressing (see page 124).

Hints and variations You can prepare this dish in advance, then just place back in the oven for 15–18 minutes to reheat and crisp the surface.

The skin, as I said, is tough. To cut it safely, rest the squash on a kitchen cloth to steady it, then use a carving knife to saw through the middle.

NATURALLY BALANCED Vitamin A comes in two forms: retinal, found in animal products, and beta-carotene, which is found in both animal and vegetable products. Both sweet potato and butternut squash are excellent sources of beta-carotene and research is proving it has a significant beneficial effect on the immune system and on growth.

Photograph opposite: Moroccan Chickpea and Coriander Casserole (see page 74) with Quinoa Grain Pilaff (see page 31).

Mackerel fillets marinated in white wine and peppercorns

*One of the most under-rated – and often the cheapest – fish on the counter,
mackerel has a unique taste and is full of goodness. Marinated overnight, the flavours
have time to penetrate deeply, so that the sharpness of the marinade marries
perfectly with the richness of the fish.*

MAKES 4 PORTIONS

4 whole mackerel, filleted

FOR THE MARINADE
120 ml/4 fl oz/½ cup water

1 carrot, thinly sliced

2 onions, thinly sliced

300 ml/½ pt/1¼ cups white wine

**100 ml/3½ fl oz/scant 1 cup
white wine vinegar**

**50 g/2 oz/¼ cup unrefined caster
(superfine) sugar**

15 ml/1 tbsp black peppercorns

15 ml/1 tbsp coriander (cilantro) seeds

1 lemon

4 bay leaves

2.5 ml/½ tsp sea salt

A pinch of saffron threads

1 Remove as many of the bones as possible from the fish. You will
need some small tweezers to remove the small pin bones. If you do
not have tweezers, a small sharp knife will help to lift them.

2 Bring the water to the boil in a saucepan, add the carrot and boil for
2 minutes. Add all the remaining marinade ingredients except the
saffron, return to the boil and boil for 1 minute. Remove from the
heat and add the saffron.

3 Lay the mackerel fillets in a large, ovenproof serving dish, pour over
the marinade and leave to cool completely.

4 Cover with clingfilm (plastic wrap) and store in the fridge for a
minimum of 4 hours, or preferably overnight.

Serving suggestions To serve cold, simply sprinkle some chopped
fresh parsley into the marinade and mix with the mackerel. it makes
a refreshing starter or, to serve as a main course, all you need to
complete the meal is some salad leaves and warm bread.
Alternatively, if you would like to serve the fish warm, simply heat the
dish in a preheated oven at 180°C/350°F/gas 4/fan oven 160°C for
about 6 minutes, then serve with new potatoes and broccoli or
Spinach Mimosa Salad (see page 25).

Hints and variations Ask your fishmonger to fillet the fish for you if
you don't have time to do it for yourself.

NATURALLY BALANCED Oily fish such as mackerel and salmon contain
large quantities of essential fatty acids as well as vitamin D, which is thought
to aid the absorption of calcium.

**Photograph opposite:
Whole Baked Chicken in a Salt Crust
Jacket (see page 78) with Sauté of
Spinach and Garlic with Lemon
(see page 86) and Farmhouse-style
Potatoes (see page 83).**

FOOD FOR FRIENDS

Moroccan chickpea and coriander casserole

Although many Moroccan dishes involve the use of an array of different spice combinations and prolonged cooking time, this version does not take much more than 20 minutes to prepare and cook. The yoghurt and herbs on top of the casserole give you a most attractive finish of red, white and green.

MAKES 4–6 PORTIONS

100 g/4 oz/⅔ cup sultanas
(golden raisins)

100 ml/3½ fl oz/scant ½ cup
kettle-hot water

15 ml/1 tbsp sunflower oil

2 onions, finely chopped

2 garlic cloves, crushed

5 ml/1 tsp ground coriander (cilantro)

5 ml/1 tsp ground cumin

2.5 ml/½ tsp cayenne

2 x 225 g/8 oz/medium cans of
chickpeas (garbanzos), drained

100 g/4 oz tomato purée (paste)

300 ml/½ pt/1¼ cups vegetable stock

1 x 225 g/8 oz/small can of
chopped tomatoes

A good pinch of sea salt

30 ml/2 tbsp plain set yoghurt

15 ml/1 tbsp chopped fresh mint
or coriander

1 Put the sultanas in a small bowl, pour over the hot water and leave to soak.

2 Heat a medium-sized flameproof casserole (Dutch oven) or tagine, then add the sunflower oil and heat. Add the onions and sauté lightly for 1 minute until transparent, then add the crushed garlic and spices and cook for a further 1 minute, stirring continuously.

3 Add the chickpeas and cook for a few minutes, stirring, so that the chickpeas absorb all the flavours.

4 Add the tomato purée and cook for a further 1 minute, stirring well until the tomato purée turns a deep ruby colour.

5 Add the vegetable stock, chopped tomatoes and the sultanas with any remaining soaking water. Bring the casserole to the boil, reduce the heat and simmer, uncovered, for 10–12 minutes. The casserole is ready once the liquid starts to thicken slightly.

6 Adjust the seasoning to taste, spoon a little yoghurt on the top and sprinkle with mint or coriander, then serve straight from the cooking pot.

Serving suggestions Roasted Spiced Couscous (see page 18) will complete this traditional Moroccan meal. It also goes well with my Quinoa Grain Pilaff (see page 31).

Hints and variations This is the perfect dish to serve straight from the cooking pot, which is why a cast-iron tagine (a North African cooking pot) is ideal. If you have a slo-cooker, you can follow the same preparation method and leave it in the slo-cooker while you are out for the day. It will not overcook and will be ready when you get home.

NATURALLY BALANCED Pulses contain a vast array of nutrients, which is why they are a very valuable part of our diet. One of the oldest foods and one of the first crops to be cultivated, traces of them have been carbon-dated to around 9750 BC – clear evidence that pulses were an important element in the diet of early humans.

Provençal fish medley with fennel and rosemary

This is a simple combination of different seafoods flavoured with the refreshing taste of fennel and rosemary. The herbs will complement any selection of fish or shellfish.

MAKES 4–6 PORTIONS

30 ml/2 tbsp cold-pressed virgin olive oil

1 onion, thinly sliced

1 medium fennel bulb, thinly sliced

2 garlic cloves, crushed

10 ml/2 tsp chopped fresh
rosemary leaves

200 g/7 oz salmon fillet

200 g/7 oz firm white fish such as
marlin, swordfish or sea bream

Sea salt and
freshly ground black pepper

6 ripe tomatoes

200 g/7 oz mussels, scrubbed
and bearded

15 ml/1 tbsp tomato purée (paste)

200 ml/7 fl oz/scant 1 cup white wine

A pinch of unrefined caster
(superfine) sugar

Juice of 1 lemon

15 ml/1 tbsp snipped fresh chives

200 g/7 oz cooked peeled prawns
(shrimp)

1 Place a large saucepan or flameproof casserole dish (Dutch oven) on a high heat and add the olive oil. Add the onion and fennel and sauté for 2 minutes, then add the garlic and rosemary and continue to cook for a further 2–3 minutes, stirring occasionally.

2 Meanwhile, remove any remaining bones and skin from the fish, and cut the fish into 1 cm/½ in chunks. Season with salt and pepper.

3 Purée the tomatoes in a food processor or liquidiser for 20–30 seconds to a coarse pulp.

4 Add the mussels, then the tomato purée and white wine to the pan and cook over a high heat, stirring well. Add the salmon and white fish, stir again, then add the blended tomatoes and a pinch of sugar. Check and adjust the seasoning if necessary.

5 Bring to the boil and add the lemon juice, half the snipped chives and finally the prawns. Stir well, then remove from the heat and cover with a lid to retain the heat until you are ready to serve.

6 Sprinkle with the remaining chives, then serve.

Serving suggestions If you are having a casual get-together, then I recommend bringing this dish to the table in the cooking pot and allowing your guests to help themselves. Serve with Lemon and Black Pepper Pilau Rice (see page 87) or warm baguettes with Tomato and Chilli Salad (see page 27).

Hints and variations To make this dish in advance, omit the chive garnish and leave it to cool. To reheat, simply cover with the lid and place on a low heat, stirring occasionally. As soon as the stew starts to boil, reduce the heat and let it simmer for 2–3 minutes until thoroughly heated through. Do not cook this dish for too long otherwise you will lose the taste and texture of the fish.

You can use raw, peeled prawns – just add them with the other fish. You can also use dried rosemary if fresh is not available, but you will only need half the quantity, or less.

NATURALLY BALANCED Seafood is packed with the mineral zinc, which is essential for the regulation of our genetic information. Zinc is also essential for the structure and function of the cell membranes. It is believed to play a significant role in the support of the immune system and is an important antioxidant, now known to be crucial for fertility and correct brain functioning.

Whole baked chicken in a salt crust jacket

The crust for this dish is not meant to be edible, it simply seals whatever you cook inside, imparting a unique flavour and aroma. When it is cooked, you can take the entire thing to the table – it looks most impressive as you cut open the crust!
See photograph opposite page 73.

MAKES 4 PORTIONS

1 lemon

50 g/2 oz/¼ cup salted butter, softened

5 ml/1 tsp dried rosemary

Freshly ground black pepper

1 x 1.5 kg/3 lb chicken

1 onion, cut into quarters

1 bay leaf

Sea salt

FOR THE SALT CRUST

900 g/2 lb/8 cups strong plain (bread) flour, plus a little more for rolling out

500 g/18 oz/2¼ cups sea salt

6 large free-range egg whites

300 ml/½ pt/1¼ cups water

15 ml/1 tbsp dried rosemary

1 large free-range egg, beaten

1 Preheat the oven to 200°C/400°F/gas 6/fan oven 180°C.

2 Grate the zest off the lemon, then cut the lemon in half.

3 Mix together the lemon zest, butter, rosemary and some black pepper and rub into the skin of the chicken. It is not necessary to use salt on the skin.

4 Stuff the cavity of the bird with the lemon halves, onion quarters and bay leaf and lightly season with a little salt. Leave to one side while you prepare the salt crust dough.

5 Mix together all the ingredients for the salt crust, except the egg, by hand or using the dough hook of your food mixer. The dough needs to be pliable but not crumbly. If the mixture is too dry, add a little more liquid but do not make it too sticky.

6 Dust the work surface with flour and roll out the dough to about 1 cm/½ in thick. Lift this dough over the chicken and then wrap completely around the bird. Make sure that there are no holes – if there are, just patch up with little bits of dough. Brush with the beaten egg to glaze.

7 Place the bird in a roasting tin (pan) and bake in the preheated oven for at least 1¾ hours until the chicken is fully cooked. To test if it is ready, simply insert a long knife into the meat between the thigh and the breast and leave for 30 seconds, then withdraw. If the knife feels hot to the touch, then the chicken is ready.

8 Remove from the oven and break open the crust with a hammer or rolling pin in front of your guests!

Serving suggestions Serve with Farmhouse-style Potatoes (see page 83) and Sauté of Spinach and Garlic (see page 86).

Hints and variations If you would like to eat the dough wrapping, then simply reduce the weight of the sea salt in the dough to 25 g/ 1 oz and add salt to the seasoning on the outside of the bird (step 3).

You can precook the chicken an hour before your guests arrive, then simply reheat it in the oven at the cooking temperature for 20–35 minutes.

NATURALLY BALANCED It is no secret that consumer demand for chicken is such that these poor animals are often fed with unnatural growth hormones to increase their size so quickly that the chickens cannot stand. For this reason, and others I have mentioned, I recommend avoiding battery chickens and opt for organic or free-range varieties.

Persian-style braised neck of lamb

This fragrant Middle Eastern dish uses one of the cheaper cuts of lamb, known as neck fillet, but despite being economical it makes a lovely dish for an informal supper with friends. I like to serve it in the cooking dish, placing it on a mat in the centre of the table surrounded by the various side dishes.

MAKES 6 PORTIONS

1 kg/2¼ lb lamb neck fillet

Sea salt and freshly ground black pepper

2 onions, chopped

75 g/3 oz/½ cup dried cranberries

2 cinnamon sticks

450 ml/¾ pt/3 cups vegetable stock

Juice of 1 lemon

100 g/4 oz/⅔ cup dried unsulphured apricots, coarsely chopped

50 g/2 oz pine nuts

1 bunch of fresh flatleaf parsley

1 Preheat the oven to 190°C/375°F/gas 5/fan oven 170°C.

2 Trim the lamb of any excess fat, then cut into slices 2 cm/¾ in thick and season generously with salt and pepper.

3 Meanwhile, heat a frying pan (skillet). Add the lamb to the pan in two batches, without any oil as there will be plenty of fat in the meat. Cook each batch over a medium to high heat for a few minutes until golden brown on all sides.

4 Remove the lamb from the pan with a slotted spoon, leaving any fat in the pan, and leave to rest on a plate.

5 Add the onions to the pan and cook for 5–6 minutes until soft, then add the cranberries and cinnamon. Add the stock and bring to the boil, scraping any sediment off the bottom of the pan into the sauce.

6 Pour this into a large, deep ovenproof dish suitable for bringing to the table, then add the lamb, lemon juice and apricots. Cover with a tight-fitting lid or foil and place the dish on a baking (cookie) tray.

7 Bake in the preheated oven for 1½ hours until the lamb is tender.

8 While the lamb is cooking, place the pine nuts on a baking tray and toast in the oven. They will take about 10–15 minutes and will turn golden brown when ready.

9 Finely chop half the flatleaf parsley. Choose the best sprigs from the other half and submerge them in water to freshen them.

10 When the lamb is cooked, remove the cinnamon sticks, stir in the chopped parsley and leave the dish to stand for 5 minutes, then garnish with the sprigs of parsley.

Serving suggestions This exotic lamb dish will go well with mashed potatoes and vegetables, but I prefer to serve the traditional accompaniment of Fluffy Basmati Rice (see page 88).

Hints and variations You can find dried cranberries in health food shops. They make ideal little sweet snacks eaten just on their own.

NATURALLY BALANCED Red meat is a good source of pantothenic acid, vitamin B5. This vitamin is believed to help boost energy levels and encourage the action of the lymphatic system, therefore improving the immune response. There is also increasing evidence that vitamin B5 may help lower cholesterol levels and protect against heart disease.

Bacon and pot barley stew cooked in ale

This lovely warming dish makes a perfect nutritious supper and the flavours of the ale and herbs give it an extra special touch. You will need a very large casserole (Dutch oven), sufficient to hold over 2½ litres/4½ pts/11 cups liquid and the bacon joint. See photograph opposite page 96.

MAKES 4–6 PORTIONS

75 g/3 oz/¾ cup pot barley

1 kg/2¼ lb bacon joint, soaked for 2–3 hours in cold water

3 medium leeks, cut into thirds

3 celery sticks, cut into thirds

3 onions, peeled and cut in half, roots left on

3 bay leaves

3 sprigs of fresh thyme or 5 ml/1 tsp dried thyme

8 black peppercorns

1 litre/1¾ pts/4¼ cups good-quality ale or stout

1 bunch of fresh parsley, coarsely chopped

1 Put the barley in a bowl, cover completely with cold water and leave to soak.

2 Rinse the soaked bacon joint, then place in a very large, deep casserole dish with all the vegetables, herbs and peppercorns. Pour in enough water to reach the top of the bacon joint. Bring to the boil, reduce the heat and simmer, uncovered, for 1 hour. If some scum rises to the surface, simply skim it off. You may need to add a little boiling water if the water reduces too much during cooking.

3 Drain the barley and add it to the pot. Pour in the ale or stout. Bring back to the boil and simmer for a further 30 minutes.

4 Lift the bacon out of the pot and leave to rest with a damp cloth over the top. Stir the parsley into the cooking liquor.

5 Slice the bacon thickly and place in a warm, deep-sided serving dish. Using a draining spoon, lift the vegetables and herbs on to the sliced bacon. Ladle over plenty of the cooking liquid and sprinkle over the toasted pine kernels before serving.

Serving suggestions Serve with Baked Butternut Squash (see page 72).

Hints and variations Try to buy pot barley as opposed to pearl, as many of the essential nutrients have been rubbed off the latter.

If you do not like thin cooking liquor, you can thicken it slightly with a little cornflour (cornstarch), mixed to a paste in 30 ml/2 tbsp of the cooking liquor.

NATURALLY BALANCED Barley is believed to benefit nerve and gall bladder function and help regulate the action of the stomach and intestines. However, it is not suitable for anyone who has colic.

Farmhouse-style potatoes

This is a traditional country-style dish that uses layers of potatoes and sautéed onions bathed in red wine and stock. The long, slow cooking gives a wonderful depth of flavour to the final dish.

See photograph opposite page 73.

MAKES 4 PORTIONS

15 ml/1 tbsp sunflower oil

2 onions

5 ml/1 tsp dried mixed herbs

400 g/14 oz potatoes, scrubbed

Sea salt and freshly ground black pepper

100 ml/3½ fl oz/scant ½ cup red wine

200 ml/7 fl oz/scant 1 cup vegetable stock

25 g/1 oz/2 tbsp salted butter

1 Preheat the oven 200°C/400°F/gas 6/fan oven 180°C.

2 Heat a medium-large frying pan (skillet) and add the oil. When it is hot, add the onions and mixed herbs and allow the onions to soften for 3–4 minutes. Once the onions have softened, season with salt and pepper and add the red wine and stock, scraping any sediment off the bottom of the pan. Remove the pan from the heat.

3 Slice the potatoes as finely as you can, using a mandolin if you have one. Place a layer of potatoes in a shallow baking dish, season lightly with salt and pepper and then spread over a little of the onion mixture. Repeat this once more, then finish with a layer of potatoes, overlapping them for an attractive finish. Dot with the butter and bake in the preheated oven for 1½ hours until crisp on top and cooked through.

Serving suggestions This dish makes an ideal accompaniment for meat and poultry dishes; try it with Whole Baked Chicken in a Salt Crust Jacket (see page 78) or my Venison Steaks with Orange, Prunes and Cinnamon (see page 122).

Hints and variations This dish takes a long time to cook and so is best placed in the bottom of the oven to cook slowly while you prepare the rest of the meal.

You can cook this dish well ahead of time, even a couple of days before you want to serve it. Try grating a little cheese over the top and turning it into a potato and cheese bake to serve with some salad for a light evening meal. You can also vary the dish, by adding extra ingredients such as bacon and herbs.

NATURALLY BALANCED Potato has the ability to neutralise body acids, which may help relieve the pain of arthritis and rheumatism.

Sag aloo

The orange juice added to this classic Indian dish enhances the flavour of the spinach, and the mustard seeds add a lovely texture to the potatoes.

MAKES 4 PORTIONS

15 ml/1 tbsp ghee or groundnut (peanut) oil

2 onions, thinly sliced

5 ml/1 tsp mustard seeds

3 large potatoes, scrubbed and diced

2 garlic cloves, crushed

10 ml/2 tsp curry powder

100 g/4 oz frozen spinach

200 ml/7 fl oz/scant 1 cup vegetable stock

200 ml/7 fl oz/scant 1 cup orange juice

Sea salt and freshly ground black pepper

1 Heat a frying pan (skillet) and add the ghee or oil. When hot, add the onions and mustard seeds and sauté for 3–4 minutes. Add the potatoes, garlic and curry powder and continue to cook for a further 2 minutes.

2 Now add the spinach to the pan with the stock and orange juice. Season with salt and pepper, then bring to a rapid boil and cook for 6–7 minutes, stirring occasionally, until the liquid has almost evaporated and the potatoes are cooked.

Serving suggestions Sag aloo will go with just about anything, from curry (of course!) to plain grilled (broiled) meat. It also tastes delicious cold – try it the next day in a lunch box.

NATURALLY BALANCED Many people suffer from indigestion after eating foods cooked in low-grade vegetable oils, which are extremely hard for the liver to break down. Ghee and groundnut oil are good choices for cooking as both can be easily absorbed by the digestive system.

Roasted sweet potatoes with coriander and cardamom

Look out for the dark, rusty-orange sweet potatoes. They have a wonderful
sweetness and leaving the skins on adds brilliant colour and texture to this dish.

MAKES 4 PORTIONS

3 sweet potatoes, scrubbed and diced

1 onion, chopped

**30 ml/2 tbsp sunflower or
groundnut (peanut) oil**

5 ml/1 tsp coriander (cilantro) seeds

5 ml/1 tsp ground cumin

2.5 ml/½ tsp ground cardamom

5 ml/1 tsp dried mixed herbs

**Sea salt and
freshly ground black pepper**

30 ml/2 tbsp chopped fresh parsley

1 Preheat the oven to 220°C/425°F/gas 7/fan oven 200°C.

2 Mix together the chopped sweet potato and onion and spread on a baking (cookie) tray. Drizzle with the oil.

3 Crush the coriander seeds with the cumin and cardamom in a pestle and mortar. Sprinkle over the potatoes with the herbs and a good pinch of salt and pepper.

4 Roast in the oven for 25–30 minutes, turning the potatoes over a couple of times to give an even colouring.

5 Transfer to a warmed serving dish and sprinkle with the parsley.

Serving suggestions These will accompany almost anything from roast meats to grilled (broiled) fish or vegetable dishes.

Hints and variations All sorts of spice combinations work well with baked sweet potatoes; lemon and mustard seeds is another good one to try, but do experiment with your own favourites.

NATURALLY BALANCED The orange flesh in sweet potatoes is a rich source of vitamin E and beta-carotene, both of which are antioxidants and are believed to help reduce the risk of cancer. Vitamin E is mainly found in fat-rich foods such as avocado, wheatgerm and butter, but sweet potatoes are low in fat, making them doubly good for you.

Carrots with orange and juniper

This is a great way to enhance the taste of this nutritious vegetable. The carrots need to be sliced as finely as you can.

MAKES 4 PORTIONS

450 g/1 lb carrots, thinly sliced

200 ml/7 fl oz/scant 1 cup
vegetable stock

Grated zest and juice of 1 orange

5 ml/1 tsp clear honey

25 g/1 oz/2 tbsp salted butter

6 juniper berries, crushed

Sea salt and
freshly ground black pepper

1 Place all the ingredients except the salt and pepper in a large saucepan, bring to a rapid boil, uncovered, then reduce the heat and simmer for about 5 minutes until the carrots are tender. You may need to add a little water to the pan if they are still crunchy in texture when the all the stock has evaporated.

2 Season the carrots with a little salt and pepper before serving.

NATURALLY BALANCED Carrots are one of the richest sources of beta-carotene, which may help reduce the risk of some cancers. They may also help clear acidic blood conditions, such as acne and rheumatism.

Sauté of spinach and garlic with lemon

Cooked spinach is often soggy, but this dish retains an appetising texture. See photograph opposite page 73.

MAKES 4 PORTIONS

25 g/1 oz/2 tbsp salted butter

2 garlic cloves, crushed

A pinch of freshly grated nutmeg

225 g/8 oz baby spinach leaves

Juice of ½ lemon

Sea salt and
freshly ground black pepper

1 Heat a large saucepan and melt the butter. Add the garlic, nutmeg and spinach leaves and stir until the leaves are coated in butter.

2 Add the lemon juice and a pinch of salt and pepper and stir well. Turn off the heat, cover with a lid and leave to stand for 5 minutes until the spinach has wilted slightly.

3 Serve warm with the liquid that is remaining at the bottom of the pan.

Serving suggestions This refreshing sauté is a particularly good accompaniment for chicken and grilled (broiled) meats.

NATURALLY BALANCED Vitamin C is water-soluble and therefore is often lost when vegetables are cooked in water, but spinach cooked this way retains more of this vitamin, as so little liquid is needed for the cooking process.

Lemon and black pepper pilau rice

This has far more flavour and texture than plain old boiled rice, but it's still amazingly quick and easy to prepare.

MAKES 4–6 PORTIONS

50 g/2 oz/¼ cup salted butter

1 cinnamon stick

1 bay leaf

10 ml/2 tsp ground turmeric

5 ml/1 tsp ground cumin

1 onion, chopped

500 g/18 oz/2¼ cups round-grain brown rice

1 litre/1¾ pts/4¼ cups vegetable stock

Juice of 1 lemon

Sea salt and freshly crushed black pepper

1 Heat the butter in a large saucepan until it sizzles, then add all the herbs and spices and cook for 1 minute to release the aromas.

2 Add the onion, turn down the heat slightly, and cook for a further 2 minutes, stirring occasionally, until softened and well blended.

3 Stir in the rice, then pour in the stock and bring to the boil. Reduce the heat, cover with a tight-fitting lid and simmer gently for about 20 minutes until the rice is just cooked.

4 Remove the cinnamon stick, season with lemon juice, salt and black pepper, and use a fork to fluff the rice slightly before serving.

Serving suggestions This rice can be served as a side dish, or you can add any leftover cooked fish, chicken or meat to make a perfect one-pot meal.

Hints and variations Add leftover cooked chicken, fish or tofu towards the end of the cooking time as that will be sufficient to reheat it – check that it is piping hot before serving.

Do try use brown rice as there is so much more flavour to the grain, although you can use long-grain white rice if you prefer (reduce the cooking time by 5 minutes). Don't grind the peppercorns too finely – they should be only coarsely crushed.

NATURALLY BALANCED Unrefined brown rice retains the nutrients in the bran layer, such as fibre and the B-vitamins, so it is much more nutritious than white rice.

Fluffy basmati rice

This cooking method makes beautifully light plain rice, which can be flavoured simply by the addition of whatever herbs you like.

MAKES 4–6 PORTIONS

450 g/1 lb/2 cups brown basmati rice

15 ml/1 tbsp sea salt

1 Rinse the rice in a sieve (strainer) under cold water until it runs clear, then place in a bowl. Fill with lukewarm water and add the salt, mixing well. Leave to soak for 1 hour to rid the rice of excess starch and help plump up the grains. This will give a really light, fluffy texture.

2 Bring a large saucepan of water with a pinch of sea salt to the boil. Drain the rice and add to the boiling water. Bring back to the boil, then reduce the heat and cook for 10–12 minutes for brown rice, 6–8 minutes for white.

3 Drain the rice, then return it to a hot, dry pan. Cover with a damp cloth and leave to rest for 10–12 minutes. It will then be completely cooked, ready for use.

Hints and variations If you want to use butter, oil or herbs to flavour the rice, add them when the rice has finished cooking (step 3) so that the flavours are absorbed while the rice is resting.

You can adjust the portions to suit whatever numbers you are cooking for; simply allow 75–100 g/3–4 oz/⅓–½ cup of rice per person.

NATURALLY BALANCED Once rice is put through a refining process, the brown husk that contains much of the essential nutrients in rice is stripped from the grain. Packed full of B-vitamins and therefore beneficial for the nervous system, brown rice is also believed to help relieve mental fatigue and depression.

food for COMFORT

Here are all those favourites that are comforting to both body and soul: hearty soups, bread, dips and desserts. Don't feel guilty about indulging yourself now and again – there are times when we need this kind of wholesome and nutritious food to make us feel better. It is also a good idea to try to make sure that mealtimes are calm events without worries, frustrations or excessive noise. Even though this can't happen all the time, try to allow yourself time to think about the food you are eating and how it is making you feel so much better. Saying grace before a meal provides a few valuable moments of reflection, and even if you are not religious, it is a good idea to begin a meal with a pause to look at and appreciate the food on your plate before you start to eat.

Broccoli buckwheat soup

The vibrant, earthy green colour of this soup is achieved by cooking the broccoli before you blend it into the soup. The buckwheat provides the deep, silky flavour and texture.

MAKES 6–8 PORTIONS

25 g/1 oz/2 tbsp salted butter

2 onions, chopped

50 g/2 oz/½ cup buckwheat flakes

5 ml/1 tsp dried mixed herbs

50 g/2 oz/½ cup ground almonds

1.5 litres/2½ pts/6 cups vegetable stock

500 g/18 oz broccoli

Sea salt and
freshly ground black pepper

100 ml/3½ fl oz/scant ½ cup plain set
Greek yoghurt

1 Heat a large saucepan, add the butter and when it has melted, add the onions, buckwheat flakes and mixed herbs. Sauté for 5–6 minutes until the onions have softened slightly.

2 Add the ground almonds and vegetable stock and bring to the boil. Turn down the heat and allow the soup to simmer for 30 minutes.

3 Bring a pan of salted water to the boil. Meanwhile, cut the broccoli into small florets and trim and finely chop some of the stem as well.

4 Blanch the broccoli in the boiling water for 3–4 minutes, then drain.

5 Add the broccoli to the soup, then blend in a liquidiser or food processor. Season to taste with salt and pepper, then add the yoghurt and mix well.

Serving suggestions Warm bread is by far the best thing to serve with this soup. A plain loaf will do, but you could also toast slices of baguette and make Garlic and Almond Butter with Tarragon (see page 125) to spread on to the warm slices.

Hints and variations Buckwheat flakes are available in health food stores and good supermarkets.

NATURALLY BALANCED Broccoli has been found to contain a powerful phytochemical called sinigrin, which is being studied because it is thought to have a deactivating effect on cancerous cells in the body.

Lebanese lentil and walnut soup

Walnuts, mint, tomatoes and lentils are all typical ingredients in Lebanese cookery. They complement each other perfectly in this soup to make a traditional and delicious meal in itself.

MAKES 4–6 PORTIONS

30 ml/2 tbsp cold-pressed virgin olive oil

1 onion, chopped

15 ml/1 tbsp cumin seeds

2.5 ml/½ tsp ground coriander (cilantro)

200 g/7 oz/1 cup puy lentils

2 garlic cloves, crushed

15 ml/1 tbsp tomato purée (paste)

1 x 225 g/8 oz/small can of chopped tomatoes

1.5 litres/2½ pts/6 cups vegetable stock

2.5 ml/½ tsp dried mint

Juice of 1 lemon

75 g/3 oz/¾ cup walnuts

Sea salt and cayenne

15 ml/1 tbsp plain yoghurt

2 tomatoes, finely chopped

15 ml/1 tbsp chopped fresh mint (optional)

1 Heat the oil in a large saucepan, then add the onion, cumin seeds and coriander and sauté for 5–6 minutes until soft.

2 Add the lentils, garlic and tomato purée and continue to cook for a further 2 minutes, stirring well.

3 Add the canned tomatoes, stock, dried mint, lemon juice and half the walnuts. Bring the soup to the boil, then reduce the heat and simmer gently for 45 minutes until the lentils are soft.

4 Meanwhile, put the remaining walnuts in a plastic bag and crush with a rolling pin. Alternatively, use a pestle and mortar.

5 Purée the soup in a food processor or liquidiser and season with plenty of salt and cayenne.

6 Spoon into suitable bowls and add a swirl of plain yoghurt to each. Serve sprinkled with crushed walnuts, chopped tomato and fresh mint, if liked.

Hints and variations You can make the soup in advance, but it will thicken a lot because of the lentils. Just thin it down with a little extra water or tomato juice.

NATURALLY BALANCED Folklore suggests that walnuts may help to ease coughing and wheezing. This link is still not scientifically proven but many people have found that it works. Walnuts have been found to help moisten the lungs and intestines.

FOOD FOR COMFORT

Miso and ginger broth

Miso, a fermented soya bean, can be found in many health food shops. There are many varieties, but I recommend using a black mugi miso paste. Miso makes a wonderful base flavour and therefore can be used to make a simple broth or added to casseroles to help give them a unique flavour.

MAKES 4–6 PORTIONS

100 g/4 oz miso paste

1 litre/1¾ pts/2½ cups kettle-hot water

2.5 cm/1 in piece of fresh root ginger, peeled and crushed

15 ml/1 tbsp chopped fresh coriander (cilantro)

3 spring onions (scallions), thinly sliced

25 g/1 oz/¼ cup sesame seeds

1 Place the miso in a medium saucepan over a low heat and pour in the hot water. It is important not to boil miso as you may destroy many of its living enzymes.

2 Whisk until the miso paste has dissolved, add the ginger, chopped coriander, spring onions and sesame seeds. Leave to infuse for 5 minutes over a very low heat.

3 Transfer the soup to warmed bowls to serve.

Serving suggestions Serve this broth as a starter, or as a refreshing savoury snack with some fine rice noodles added, if liked.

NATURALLY BALANCED Miso has a settling action on the stomach and therefore is excellent for anyone feeling a little poorly. It is highly praised in Japan for its health-promoting qualities. Studies have shown that local people who ate a diet rich in soya and miso were more likely to survive radiation sickness after the nuclear explosions in Hiroshima and Nagasaki at the end of the Second World War. The soya was believed to help absorb and carry radiation out of the body, although this is still not scientifically proven.

Yellow split pea soup with paprika yoghurt

Yellow spilt peas are a perfect comfort food, as well as being economical to buy, easy to store and full of nutritional value. They have a smooth and velvety texture once cooked, and a delicious creamy taste.

MAKES 6–8 PORTIONS

50 g/2 oz/¼ cup salted butter

2 onions, thinly sliced

2 carrots, thinly sliced

5 ml/1 tsp ground turmeric

2.5 ml/½ tsp ground cumin

2.5 ml/½ tsp ground cloves

250 g/9 oz/1½ cups yellow split peas

3 garlic cloves, finely crushed

1.5 litres/2½ pts/6 cups vegetable stock

**Sea salt and
freshly ground black pepper**

FOR THE GARNISH
15 ml/1 tbsp chopped fresh parsley

5 ml/1 tsp paprika

A pinch of cayenne

**200 ml/7 fl oz/scant 1 cup plain set
Greek yoghurt**

1 Set a large saucepan over a medium to high heat and add the butter. Once it has melted, add the onions, carrots and spices and sauté for 3–4 minutes.

2 Add the yellow split peas and garlic and continue to sauté over a low heat for a further 5 minutes.

3 Add the stock and seasoning, bring to the boil, then reduce the heat, cover and simmer gently for 40–45 minutes.

4 Meanwhile, mix together the parsley, paprika and cayenne – add more cayenne if you like your food very hot – then combine with the Greek yoghurt.

5 Once the soup has finished cooking, remove from the heat and purée in a liquidiser or food processor. Be careful, as the soup will be very hot.

6 Taste and adjust the seasoning with salt and pepper, then serve in bowls with the paprika yoghurt swirled on top.

Serving suggestions Serve the soup with crusty home-made bread.

Hints and variations You can easily make the soup in bulk, then pour it into small containers for freezing.

NATURALLY BALANCED A thick, wholesome soup is a perfect meal to eat if you get home from work late, as it is easy for the digestive organs to absorb the nutrients. Eating heavy, starchy meals late at night puts excess strain on the organs at a time when the body is starting to wind down, which can create bowel problems.

Butter bean and tomato pâté with hazelnuts

Hazelnuts (filberts) and butter (lima) beans have always been a great marriage. In this pâté I have incorporated the acidity of tomatoes to help counterbalance the richness of the hazelnuts.

MAKES 4–6 PORTIONS

100 g/4 oz/1 cup hazelnuts

1 x 225 g/8 oz/small can of butter beans, drained

2 garlic cloves, crushed

2 ripe tomatoes, roughly chopped

15 ml/1 tbsp tomato purée (paste)

Grated zest and juice of 1 lemon

2.5 ml/½ tsp ground coriander (cilantro)

15 ml/1 tbsp tahini (sesame paste)

15 ml/1 tbsp Worcestershire sauce

5 ml/1 tsp Dijon mustard

30 ml/2 tbsp hazelnut oil

1 bunch of fresh coriander, finely chopped

A pinch of ground cumin

2.5 ml/½ tsp sea salt

A pinch of cayenne

1 Preheat the grill (broiler) to maximum.

2 Place the hazelnuts on a baking (cookie) tray under the grill and toast for 4–5 minutes until golden brown.

3 Place half the hazelnuts in a food processor and blend until finely broken down. Add the butter beans, garlic, tomatoes, tomato purée, lemon juice, ground coriander, tahini, Worcestershire sauce and mustard and blend until all the ingredients are mixed together. Gradually add the hazelnut oil, then half of the chopped coriander and the cumin, salt and cayenne. Scoop the pâté into a serving dish.

4 Place the remaining hazelnuts in a bag with the lemon zest and beat with a rolling pin until coarsely crushed. Mix the crushed nuts with the remaining coriander, then sprinkle over the pâté before serving.

Serving suggestions Serve with fresh warm bread or spread on toasted bagels or in sandwiches. This pâté can also be served individually in ramekins (custard cups) with the nut mixture spread over the top.

Hints and variations You can make the pâté in advance and leave it in the fridge for up to three days before serving. Take it out of the fridge 30 minutes before serving to allow the flavours to develop. It does not freeze well.

NATURALLY BALANCED Hazelnuts are surprisingly high in calcium compared to many other nuts. Calcium is essential not only to the building and maintenance of the bones and teeth, but also to help nerve and muscle function. There is good evidence to suggest that calcium can reduce the risk of bowel cancer.

Home-made hummus with fresh mint

The advantage of making your own hummus is that you avoid the low-grade vegetable oil that most commercially available hummus contains and you can add whatever you like to flavour the basic components. For this recipe I have added fresh mint, which I think makes a truly delicious dip.

MAKES 4–6 PORTIONS

1 x 225 g/8 oz/small can of chickpeas (garbanzos), drained

30 ml/2 tbsp tahini (sesame paste)

Juice of 2 lemons

2.5 ml/½ tsp ground cumin

2 garlic cloves, crushed

A pinch of sea salt

A pinch of cayenne

45 ml/3 tbsp cold-pressed virgin olive oil

15 ml/1 tbsp kettle-hot water

15 ml/1 tbsp chopped fresh mint (optional)

1 Place the chickpeas in a food processor with the tahini, lemon juice, cumin, garlic, salt and cayenne and blend together.

2 Gradually add the olive oil and hot water very slowly. Once all the liquid has been added, check the texture and if it is still too thick, then add a little more water. Hummus should be a little runny.

3 Adjust the seasoning and finally stir in the chopped fresh mint.

Serving suggestions Garnish the hummus with stoned (pitted) olives, a sprinkling of paprika and lemon wedges. Hummus is delicious served with any warm bread, but for a really authentic feast, try making Home-made Pitta Breads (see page 106). You could also complement the hummus with Roasted Aubergine and Tahini Dip (see page 96), and serve a little bowl of high-quality cold-pressed olive oil to dip vegetables and bread into.

NATURALLY BALANCED Because of the combination of cereals and pulses – sesame and chickpeas – hummus is an extremely good source of complete protein for vegetarians. Although hummus is high in calories, due to the oil content, all the ingredients are beneficial to the maintenance of the body.

Roasted aubergine and tahini dip

Comforting and delicious, you can make this smooth, creamy dip as hot and spicy or mild and delicate as you like.

MAKES 8 PORTIONS

1 medium to large aubergine (eggplant)

60 ml/4 tbsp cold-pressed virgin olive oil

5 ml/1 tsp ground cumin

5 ml/1 tsp paprika

2.5 ml/½ tsp cayenne

15 ml/1 tbsp tahini (sesame paste)

5 ml/1 tsp organic crunchy peanut butter

Juice of 1 lemon

200 ml/7 fl oz/scant 1 cup plain set Greek yoghurt

1 bunch of fresh coriander (cilantro), chopped

Sea salt and freshly ground black pepper

1 Preheat the oven to 200°C/400°F/gas 6/fan oven 180°C.

2 Cut the aubergine in half lengthways, then use a small knife to score the inside with a 'criss-cross' pattern. Place the halves on a baking (cookie) tray.

3 Mix the olive oil with the cumin, paprika and cayenne and pour over the tops of the aubergine halves.

4 Bake in the preheated oven for 25–30 minutes until the flesh is soft to the touch.

5 Scoop out the flesh using a spoon and place in a liquidiser or food processor. Add the tahini, peanut butter, lemon juice and yoghurt and blend to a purée, then add the chopped coriander at the last minute. Season to taste with salt and pepper and serve.

Serving suggestions This aubergine dip makes an excellent simple starter with some home-made bread. It is also delicious spread in sandwiches or on crispbreads, or served as part of a light lunch or buffet, with sticks of raw vegetables.

Hints and variations The dip does not freeze well, but will keep in the fridge for a couple of days.

NATURALLY BALANCED Aubergines soak oil up like sponges and quite often people cook aubergines in far too much oil because of this. It is best to dust them with a little flour so that oil will not be absorbed so easily and you will retain the beautiful, delicate taste of aubergine.

**Photograph opposite:
Bacon and Barley Stew
Cooked in Ale (see page 82).**

Curried peanut butter and mango dip

Groundnuts (peanuts) and curry spices have been used together for centuries in many parts of the world as a classic flavour combination. This recipe makes a delicious dip or spread, with the mango chutney giving a contrast of texture and a little sweetness.

MAKES 6 PORTIONS

125 g/4½ oz/generous ½ cup organic crunchy peanut butter

30 ml/2 tbsp coconut milk

30 ml/2 tbsp groundnut (peanut) oil

75 g/3 oz/¼ cup mango chutney, smooth or chunky

15 ml/1 tbsp Worcestershire sauce

5 ml/1 tsp mild curry paste

Juice of 1 lemon

1 Put all the ingredients in a liquidiser or food processor and blend until the mixture is thoroughly smooth.

2 Pour into a small serving bowl and chill until required.

Serving suggestions You can serve this simply as a dip with warmed Home-made Pitta Breads (see page 106), cut into long fingers.

Hints and variations This dip works well as a filling for baked potatoes. Try it also with baked yellow sweet potatoes, which are widely available in supermarkets.

NATURALLY BALANCED Peanuts are often heavily sprayed and grown on land saturated with synthetic fertilisers, and they are also susceptible to the carcinogenic fungus aflatoxin. Organically grown peanuts are subject to far fewer chemical residues and also more resistant to aflatoxin.

**Photograph opposite:
Warm Duck Salad with Crispy
Skin and Peaches (see page 121).**

Grated beetroot and apple salad

The humble beetroot (red beet) is grossly under-rated as a vegetable. It marries well with the taste of apple and in this recipe horseradish gives a slight sharpness to the finished salad, which makes a delicious starter or a snack for any time of day. You can use either raw or cooked beetroot, according to your preference.

MAKES 4 PORTIONS

4 medium beetroots, raw or cooked

2 dessert (eating) apples

Juice of ½ lemon

100 g/4 oz/1 cup walnuts, coarsely crushed

30 ml/2 tbsp crème fraîche or plain set yoghurt

10 ml/2 tsp creamed horseradish

Sea salt and freshly ground black pepper

1 If you are using raw beetroots, then give them a good wash and scrub. Whether raw or cooked, peel then coarsely grate them into a large mixing bowl.

2 Peel, core and coarsely grate the apples into the same bowl.

3 Add the lemon juice, half the crushed walnuts, the crème fraîche or yoghurt and the creamed horseradish and mix together well. Season to taste with salt and pepper.

4 Tip the mixture into individual salad bowls or one large serving bowl and sprinkle with the remaining walnuts.

Serving suggestions This delicious mixture can be served as a simple snack, piled on oatcakes. Alternatively, serve it as a side dish with fish, such as grilled (broiled) salmon or baked trout or as part of a selection of salads for a buffet or barbecue.

NATURALLY BALANCED Beetroot is one of nature's most colourful vegetables and also one of the most richest vegetable sources of folic acid. This essential vitamin is needed for the production of DNA and helps to boost the immune system. There is also a well-documented tradition that suggests beetroot may relieve constipation.

FOOD FOR COMFORT

Curried broccoli fritters with dipping sauce

These crunchy snacks are complemented perfectly by the sweet yet tangy sauce that accompanies them – a real treat for all lovers of spicy food.

MAKES 12–14 FRITTERS
Groundnut oil, for deep-frying

200 g/7 oz/1¾ cups unbleached self-raising (self-rising) flour

10 ml/2 tsp medium curry powder

300 ml/½ pt/1¼ cups lager

2 medium heads of broccoli, cut into florets

Sea salt

FOR THE DIPPING SAUCE
30 ml/2 tbsp white wine vinegar

45 ml/3 tbsp unrefined caster (superfine) sugar

1 red chilli, seeded and finely chopped

15 ml/1 tbsp soy sauce

1 Heat the oil in a deep-fat fryer or large, heavy-based saucepan to 190°C/375°F, when a cube of day-old bread will brown in 30 seconds.

2 While it heats, make the batter. Place the flour and curry powder in a bowl and slowly whisk in the lager.

3 Using tongs, dip the broccoli florets into the batter, then lower gently into the hot oil a few at a time. Cook until they are golden and float to the surface, then remove from the oil, drain well on kitchen paper (paper towels) and sprinkle with a little salt.

4 To prepare the dressing, place the vinegar and sugar in a small pan with the chilli and bring to the boil. Remove from the heat and add the soy sauce.

5 Place the broccoli florets on a warm serving platter and serve with the dressing.

Serving suggestions Try serving these little broccoli fritters with other sauces such as Sweet Tomato Dressing (see page 128).

Hints and variations You can make the fritters in advance if you would like to get the work out of the way, then pop them back into the hot oil for a minute to reheat when you are ready to serve.

NATURALLY BALANCED When you heat cooking oil, the molecules start to move more energetically, thus causing friction that creates heat. The hotter the oil gets, the more friction there is and therefore more heat, until the oil smokes and oxidises. This is the point at which the oil releases harmful toxins known as free radicals. Groundnut oil oxidises at a much higher temperature and is therefore less harmful than many other cooking oils.

Baked avocado with a stilton crust

Although avocado and Stilton are both rich flavours, they harmonise very well together. This simple dish is a lovely way of serving avocado warm: although the avocado is baked it still keeps its creamy texture and taste. Choose avocados that are ripe but still firm.

MAKES 4 PORTIONS

4 medium avocados

Juice of ½ lemon

150 ml/¼ pt/⅝ cup crème fraîche

75 g/3 oz/¾ cup Stilton cheese, crumbled

50 g/2 oz/½ cup fresh breadcrumbs

50 g/2 oz/½ cup flaked (slivered) almonds

15 ml/1 tbsp chopped fresh parsley

30 ml/2 tbsp cold-pressed virgin olive oil

Sea salt and freshly ground black pepper

1 Preheat the oven to 200°C/400°F/gas 6/fan oven 180°C.

2 Cut each avocado in half, remove the stone (pit) and gently peel off the skin. Cut a tiny slice off the rounded side of each avocado so that they don't roll around, and place them on a baking (cookie) tray.

3 Brush each avocado all over with a little lemon juice, then fill the inside with crème fraîche.

4 Mix together the Stilton, breadcrumbs, almonds, parsley and oil and season with salt and pepper. Make sure all the ingredients have bound together.

5 Place a spoonful of the mixture on each avocado and spread lightly to cover the entire surface.

6 Bake in the oven for 12–14 minutes until the Stilton crust starts to turn slightly golden brown.

7 Serve on warm individual plates.

Serving suggestions These go very well with Sweet Tomato Dressing (see page 128) or either of my coleslaws (see pages 22 and 23). You can serve them as a light lunch or supper, or just prepare half an avocado per person and serve as an impressive starter.

Hints and variations Because the lemon juice stops the avocado from going brown, you can prepare this recipe in advance, even the night before, and then place in the oven when you are ready to start preparing the meal.

NATURALLY BALANCED Avocados are known to be great brain food – anyone revising for exams please note! This is because among the many nutrients they contain is lecithin, which is essential for proper brain functioning.

Simple creamy mashed potatoes

Mashed potatoes are a real old favourite and can be teamed with just about anything. For best results, choose a good-quality, floury potato, such as Maris Piper or King Edward.

MAKES 4–6 PORTIONS

1 kg/2¼ lb potatoes, diced

200 ml/7 fl oz/scant 1 cup milk

50 g/2 oz/¼ cup salted butter

A pinch of cayenne

A little sea salt

1 Place the potatoes in a saucepan and cover with lightly salted water. Bring to the boil, then reduce the heat, cover and simmer for about 20 minutes until tender.

2 Drain, then return to the same pan. Cook over a very low heat for a couple of minutes to dry the potatoes while you stir and mash them.

3 Add the milk and butter and season to taste with cayenne and salt, mashing the ingredients well into the potatoes until they are soft and fluffy, and adding a little extra milk if necessary to reach the consistency you prefer.

Serving suggestions There are really no limits to what goes well with mashed potato, although I think it is particularly good served with sausages or casseroles. If left to cool slightly, you can use this as a base for making potato cakes and patties.

NATURALLY BALANCED Try making mashed potatoes with their skins left on. Not only does this help retain their excellent source of fibre and B-vitamins, but it also provides a wonderful taste and texture to the mash.

Broccoli and almond mash

Broccoli and almond is one of the classic culinary combinations, and adding these delicious ingredients to good old mashed potato creates a really delicious all-in-one vegetable and potato dish.

MAKES 4–6 PORTIONS

1 kg/2¼ lb potatoes, peeled and diced

2 heads of broccoli, cut into small florets

200 ml/7 fl oz/scant 1 cup milk

50 g/2 oz/¼ cup salted butter

75 g/3 oz/¾ cup ground almonds

15 ml/1 tbsp Dijon mustard

¼ nutmeg, finely grated

A pinch of cayenne

A little sea salt

30 ml/2 tbsp toasted flaked (slivered) almonds

1 Place the potatoes in a saucepan and cover with lightly salted water. Bring to the boil, then reduce the heat, cover and simmer for about 15 minutes. Add the broccoli, then boil for a further 6 minutes until the vegetables are tender.

2 Drain, then return to the same pan. Cook over a very low heat for a couple of minutes to dry the potatoes and broccoli, stirring and mashing at the same time.

3 Add the milk, butter, ground almonds, mustard and nutmeg and season to taste with cayenne and salt, mashing the ingredients well into the potatoes.

4 Turn into a warmed serving dish and garnish with the flaked almonds.

Serving suggestions Use this mash recipe to accompany my Baked Salmon (see page 120) or try it with my Venison Steaks (see page 122). Alternatively, you could enjoy a bowl on its own, just with Caramelised Onion Sauce (see page 124).

NATURALLY BALANCED Always cook broccoli for the shortest possible time, as its vitamin C content is destroyed by boiling.

Carmel's soda bread

*This is as traditional as Irish soda bread can get. The recipe was passed on to me by
an excellent Irish chef. Although Carmel and many other Irish chefs like her would
insist on making fresh soda bread each day, I would recommend making a little extra
and freezing it, just in case you get peckish late at night!*

MAKES 2 LARGE SODA BREAD CAKES

200 g/7 oz/1¾ cups rolled porridge oats

**700 g/1½ lb/6 cups wholemeal plain
(all-purpose) flour**

**450 g/1 lb/4 cups unbleached
self-raising (self-rising) flour**

**10 ml/2 tsp bicarbonate of soda
(baking soda)**

10 ml/2 tsp sea salt

2 large free-range eggs, beaten

850 ml/1⅓ pts/3½ cups buttermilk

1 Preheat the oven to 200°C/400°F/gas 6/fan oven 180°C and grease
a baking (cookie) tray.

2 Reserve half the oats for rolling out the dough, then place all the
remaining dry ingredients in a bowl.

3 Add the eggs and buttermilk and knead very lightly until the mixture
begins to pull together.

4 Dust a clean work surface with the reserved porridge oats, tip out
the mixture and bring it together with your hands to form a ball, then
cut in half. Shape into two round cakes and place on the baking tray.
Using a palette knife, score a cross on each loaf to define the
wedges.

5 Bake in the preheated oven for 20 minutes, then reduce the oven
temperature to 160°C/325°F/gas 3/fan oven 145°C and cook for a
further 20 minutes until the loaves sound hollow when tapped on the
base.

6 Remove from the oven and leave to cool on a wire rack.

Serving suggestions For breakfast, to accompany a rustic soup, or
just spread with a little butter for a snack – this bread is delicious
served any way you like.

Hints and variations You can usually buy buttermilk in the
supermarket, but if you can't find it, simply leave some milk out
overnight in a warm place. Alternatively, use half milk and half plain
live yoghurt.

NATURALLY BALANCED Buttermilk contains very little fat – it is the liquid that
can often be seen if you over-whip cream.

American-style corn bread

The Americans often use chilli to give a bit of spice to their corn bread, but you can just omit this if you don't fancy it – the recipe will be equally delicious. If you have the time to scrape the kernels off fresh corn cobs, that will give an even better flavour than canned kernels.

MAKES 1 x 900 G/2 LB LOAF

150 g/5 oz/1¼ cups unbleached self-raising (self-rising) flour

175 g/6 oz/1½ cups cornmeal

50 g/2 oz/½ cup mature Cheddar cheese, grated

2 red chillies, seeded and finely chopped

25 g/1 oz/2 tbsp unrefined caster (superfine) sugar

2.5 ml/½ tsp ground cumin

2.5 ml/½ tsp ground coriander (cilantro)

1 x 200 g/7 oz/small can of sweetcorn (corn)

150 ml/¼ pt/⅔ cup plain yoghurt

100 ml/3½ fl oz/scant ½ cup milk

2 medium free-range eggs, beaten

1 Preheat the oven to 190°C/375°F/gas 5/fan oven 170°C and grease and line a 900 g/2 lb loaf tin (pan).

2 Place the flour, cornmeal, half the grated cheese, the chillies, sugar, cumin and coriander in bowl.

3 Blend together the sweetcorn, yoghurt, milk and eggs in a liquidiser or food processor. Pour on to the dry ingredients and mix well.

4 Spoon the mixture into the prepared tin and sprinkle with the remaining cheese.

5 Bake in the preheated oven for 1 hour until set in the middle.

6 Remove the hot corn bread from the tin and leave to cool.

Serving suggestions Corn bread is delicious served with any soups and dips and I like it with Tomato and Chilli Salad (see page 27). It is also perfect served with a well-flavoured, marinated salmon, such as my Bourbon-marinated Salmon (see page 116).

NATURALLY BALANCED Maize is just another name for corn, so maize meal and cornmeal are the same. Corn is a very nutritious food and was the staple food of the native Americans. It helps to cleanse the kidneys and promotes healthy teeth and gums.

Malted sunflower and linseed bread

This is really easy to prepare as the recipe uses dried yeast and the dough only needs to rise once before baking, rather than having to go through the lengthy process of double fermentation.

MAKES 2 x 900 G/2 LB LOAVES

A little sunflower oil, for greasing

500 g/18 oz/4½ cups wholemeal bread (strong) flour

500 g/18 oz/4½ cups strong white (bread) flour

2 sachets of easy-blend dried yeast

5 ml/1 tsp sea salt

30 ml/2 tbsp malt extract or black treacle (molasses)

50 g/2 oz/½ cup sunflower seeds

50 g/2 oz/½ cup linseeds

750 ml/1¼ pts/3 cups lukewarm water

15 ml/1 tbsp milk, for brushing

1 Preheat the oven to 200°C/400°F/gas 6/fan oven 180°C.

2 Grease two 900 g/2 lb loaf tins (pans) with a little sunflower oil.

3 Mix together the flours, yeast and salt in a large mixing bowl, then stir in the malt or treacle and seeds. Slowly add the lukewarm water, mixing with your hand until you have a soft dough. Alternatively, use a food processor or mixer with a dough hook to make the dough.

4 Continue to knead for 5–6 minutes until the dough is pliable and no longer sticky.

5 Divide the dough in half and press into the greased tins, then cover and leave in a warm place to rise for 20 minutes.

6 Gently brush the tops of the loaves with milk, then bake in the preheated oven for 20 minutes. Reduce the oven temperature to 190°C/375°F/gas 5/fan oven 170°C and continue to cook for a further 15 minutes until the loaves sound hollow when tapped on the base.

7 Remove from the tins and leave to cool on a wire rack.

Serving suggestions Serve warm with some home-made soup, or my Roasted Aubergine and Tahini Dip (see page 96).

Hints and variations The bread freezes very well, but this is best done as soon as it cools or the next day at the latest. Linseeds are available in health food shops.

NATURALLY BALANCED Many people feel bloated and tired after eating wheat products, and this is believed to be caused by the over-consumption of refined rancid gluten, which is added to commercially baked breads, pasties and pizzas to lighten the dough and prolong its shelf life. Making your own bread can help to avoid such problems.

Home-made pitta breads

Pitta breads can be enjoyed with all sorts of dishes, whatever their origin, and are very simple to make.

MAKES 4–6

100 g/4 oz/1 cup wholemeal strong plain (bread) flour

350 g/12 oz/3 cups white strong plain (bread) flour

1 sachet of easy-blend dried yeast

5 ml/1 tsp sea salt

5 ml/1 tsp unrefined caster (superfine) sugar

300 ml/½ pt/1¼ cups lukewarm water

A little sunflower oil, for brushing

1 Combine the flours, yeast, salt and sugar in a mixing bowl. Add the water and mix until you have a soft but not sticky dough.

2 Turn out the dough on to a lightly floured surface and knead vigorously for 5 minutes.

3 Put the dough back into a floured bowl, cover and leave to rise for 30 minutes.

4 Knock back (punch down) the dough and knead again for a good 5 minutes, while you heat either a griddle pan or your grill (broiler) to maximum temperature.

5 Roll out the dough with a rolling pin on a floured surface. Cut circles out with a knife or a cutter. Brush each one with a little oil on both sides.

6 Cook on the griddle pan or under the grill for 3 minutes on each side until puffed up and spotted with brown. They are best served warm.

Serving suggestions You can serve pitta breads as an accompaniment to soups, salads or main courses, or cut them into strips to serve with dips. My Rillette of Avocado (see page 114) makes an excellent filling, spooned into split pitta 'pockets'.

Hints and variations Pitta breads freeze well and can be defrosted in the microwave on Full Power for about 1 minute per bread if you are in a hurry.

Traditional naan breads

Indian naan breads need not be reserved just to serve with curry – although, of course, they are perfect for that!

MAKES ABOUT 4

250 g/9 oz/2¼ cups unbleached self-raising (self-rising) flour

30 ml/2 tbsp plain live yoghurt

15 ml/1 tbsp icing (confectioners') sugar

5 ml/1 tsp ground coriander (cilantro)

5 ml/1 tsp sea salt

120 ml/4 fl oz/½ cup lukewarm water

1 Put the flour, yoghurt, sugar, coriander and salt into a large mixing bowl. Add the measured water a little at a time, working it into the flour with your fingers. Bring the mixture together, adding just enough water to make a soft, slightly sticky dough.

2 Knead the dough roughly for a minute until well blended, then cover with a damp tea towel (dish cloth) and leave in a warm spot for about 1 hour for the dough to ferment.

3 Pull off a small piece of dough with floured fingers, shape it into a ball, then roll out on a floured surface to an oval shape. Repeat with the remaining dough.

4 Heat a griddle pan or grill (broiler) and cook the naan breads for about 30 seconds on each side until they puff up and are speckled with black spots. Serve warm.

Serving suggestions As well as curries, naan are great with dips and salads, or try them with Sag Aloo (see page 84).

Hints and variations Naan breads freeze well and can be defrosted the microwave on Full Power for about 1 minute per bread. Alternatively, just leave them at room temperature for an hour or so.

Earl grey fruit teacake

This is my grandma's recipe. It is completely fat free – although my grandma always serves it sliced and thickly coated in fresh butter, but who can blame her! It is worth soaking the fruit for at least four hours, so I usually plan ahead and soak it overnight ready to bake the cake the next day.

MAKES 1 x 900 G/2 LB LOAF

275 g/10 oz/1¾ cups dried mixed fruit (fruit cake mix)

150 g/5 oz/⅔ cup soft brown sugar

Finely grated zest and juice of 2 oranges

150 ml/¼ pt/⅔ cup of very strong Earl Grey tea

1 large free-range egg, beaten

275 g/10 oz/2½ cups unbleached self-raising (self-rising) flour

1 Soak the fruit, sugar and orange zest in the orange juice and tea for at least 4 hours.

2 Preheat the oven to 150°C/300°F/gas 2/fan oven 135°C and grease and line a 900 g/2 lb loaf tin (pan).

3 Add the egg and flour to the fruit mixture and mix thoroughly. Spoon the mixture into the prepared tin.

4 Bake in the preheated oven for 1½ hours. The cake is ready when a small knife inserted in the centre comes out clean.

Serving suggestions Slice thinly and spread with softened fresh butter – it's hard to beat this, but you might like to try coating it with plain cream cheese for a really delicious snack. It goes without mention that this teacake is best served with a pot of Earl Grey!

Hints and variations You can use a 20 cm/8 in cake tin if you prefer.

NATURALLY BALANCED Some dried fruit in supermarkets is sprayed with liquid paraffin, a petrol derivative, to give the fruits an attractive, glossy shine, but this can cause indigestion. You can avoid this by buying your dried fruits in your local health food shop.

Carrot and apricot cake with mascarpone icing

Carrot cake is always a great favourite. This recipe uses both apricots and orange whose sweetness helps to reduce the sugar content, and using one part of wholemeal (wholewheat) and two parts of white flour is a good way of making the cake really nutritious without being heavy.

MAKES 1 x 20 CM/8 IN CAKE

1 orange

1 lemon

100 g/4 oz/⅔ cup dried unsulphured apricots, chopped

50 g/2 oz/½ cup wholemeal plain (all-purpose) flour

150 g/6 oz/1½ cups unbleached self-raising (self-rising) flour

5 ml/1 tsp ground mixed (apple-pie) spice

5 ml/1 tsp ground cinnamon

5 ml/1 tsp bicarbonate of soda (baking soda)

175 g/6 oz/¾ cup muscovado sugar

3 large free-range eggs, beaten

150 ml/¼ pt/⅔ cup sunflower oil

1000 g/4 oz/1 cup walnuts, broken into pieces

175 g/6 oz carrots, finely grated

225 g/8 oz/1 cup mascarpone cheese

15 ml/1 tbsp clear honey

1 Preheat the oven to 160°C/325°F/gas 3/fan oven 145°C and grease and line a deep 20 cm/8 in cake tin (pan). Grate the zest from the orange and lemon and reserve. Squeeze the juice from both fruit.

2 Place the apricots, orange juice and lemon juice in a small saucepan and bring to the boil, then turn off the heat and leave to soak for a few minutes.

3 Mix the flours, spices and bicarbonate of soda in a large mixing bowl. Beat in the sugar, eggs and sunflower oil until completely smooth. Reserve about 10 pieces of walnut for decoration and stir the remainder into the mixture with the carrots and mix until all the ingredients are well blended. Pour the mixture into the prepared tin.

4 Bake in the preheated oven for about 1½ hours until well risen and firm to the touch.

5 Turn out on to a wire rack, remove the lining paper and leave to cool.

6 Beat together the mascarpone cheese and honey with the reserved zest of the orange and lemon. Spread evenly over the cooled cake using a palette knife, then press a fork all over the surface to give the cake a rustic finish. Decorate with the reserved walnut pieces.

Hints and variations Because of the topping on this cake, it will need to be stored in the fridge. It will also freeze for a month.

NATURALLY BALANCED Everyone enjoys a slice of cake now and then, and there is nothing wrong with that as part of a healthy, balanced diet. Remember, though, that it is better to make your own, as many commercially made cakes contain hydrogenated fat to help extend their shelf life and research now suggests that this chemically altered fat can be toxic as the body is not able to deal with it.

Baked cheesecake with walnuts and stem ginger

Baked cheesecakes are extremely easy to prepare and I personally think that they have a better flavour and texture than their unbaked counterparts. Preserved stem ginger makes a wonderful partner to cream cheese, and here it is rounded off with the mellow taste of walnuts.

MAKES 6–8 PORTIONS

FOR THE BASE

100 g/4 oz ginger biscuits (cookies)

50 g/2 oz/½ cup walnuts

75 g/3 oz/⅓ cup unsalted (sweet) butter

A pinch of ground ginger

FOR THE FILLING

150 g/5 oz stem ginger, drained, reserving the juice, and finely chopped

400 g/14 oz/1¾ cups plain full-fat cream cheese

400 ml/14 oz/1¾ cups plain Greek yoghurt or fromage frais

2 large free-range eggs

100 g/4 oz/½ cup unrefined caster (superfine) sugar

1.5 ml/¼ tsp vanilla essence (extract)

Grated zest of ½ lemon

50 g/2 oz/½ cup walnuts

1 Preheat the oven to 160°C/325°F/gas 3/fan oven 145°C and grease and line a 20 cm/8 in loose-based or springform cake tin (pan).

2 To make the base, crush the ginger biscuits and walnuts in a food processor, or place them in a bag and crush them with a rolling pin. Don't worry if there are a few lumps as they add texture.

3 Melt the butter with the ground ginger, then stir in the biscuit mixture. Press into the prepared cake tin.

4 Put all the filling ingredients into the food processor and mix well, then pour over the biscuit base.

5 Bake in the preheated oven for 30–35 minutes until the filling has set. You can check this by gently pressing your finger in the middle to test – it should feel firm to the touch but still give a little.

6 Leave to cool in the tin for at least 4 hours, preferably overnight. Once cooled, ease a knife down the side of the tin and remove the cheesecake.

7 Decorate with pieces of stem ginger and chopped walnuts. Mix the icing sugar and ginger, if using, and dust over the top. Put the reserved syrup from the stem ginger into a small bowl with the lemon juice and sweeten to taste. Stir the mixture, then drizzle over the cheesecake.

TO FINISH

A few pieces of stem ginger

30 ml/2 tbsp chopped walnuts

30 ml/2 tbsp icing (confectioner's) sugar

A pinch of ground ginger (optional)

Juice of ½ lemon

A pinch of unrefined caster sugar

Serving suggestion Cut the cheesecake into slices. Place each slice on a plate dusted with more ginger and icing sugar. Serve with fresh strawberries or raspberries in the summer and stewed fruit as a winter dessert.

Hints and variations You can prepare this cheesecake in advance and store in the fridge overnight, but it is best brought out for 1 hour before serving to bring out the subtle flavours.

NATURALLY BALANCED Walnuts are rich in omega-3, the essential fat required by the brain in order to perform and transform correct chemical responses and sequences.

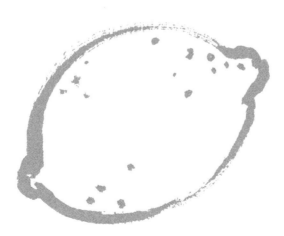

food to
IMPRESS

Cooking to impress requires absolute harmony. Plan ahead, and think about who you are cooking for, the combination of ingredients, what you are going to prepare and how you are going to present the food. That way, you will have everything sorted out in advance and avoid getting too anxious. The important thing is that you stay calm and keep your attention focused on the food.

Think carefully about presentation: a dish that is a delight to the nose and the eyes will be welcomed by your guests and will put them in the right frame of mind even before they have taken a mouthful.

You'll find ideas here for starters, main courses and desserts together with sauces and dressings that will show you how to combine flavours, textures and tastes to enhance and balance your cooking.

Marinated prawn cocktail with allspice and mango

This makes an extremely refreshing and colourful starter that would also suit a light lunch for two. It's a much lighter version of the classic prawn (shrimp) cocktail, whose subtle flavours are often drowned in a mayonnaise-based dressing.

MAKES 4 PORTIONS

400 g/14 oz cooked peeled prawns

2 limes

1 ripe mango

1 red onion, finely chopped

45 ml/3 tbsp cold-pressed virgin olive oil

A good pinch of ground allspice

1 red chilli, seeded

A pinch of unrefined caster (superfine) sugar

Sea salt and freshly ground black pepper

15 ml/1 tbsp chopped fresh coriander (cilantro)

100 g/4 oz baby spinach leaves

1 Mix the prawns with the juice of one of the limes and leave in the fridge while you prepare the dressing.

2 Peel, stone (pit) and cut the mango into small dice. Mix with the juice of the remaining lime, the onion, oil and allspice and leave to infuse.

3 Finely chop the chilli with the sugar (this will take a little of the heat out of the chilli). Mix with the mango and onion, season to taste and finish by adding the chopped fresh coriander.

4 Mix half of the dressing with the prawns and reserve the other half.

5 Make a bed of spinach leaves in the centre of a serving platter and pile a mound of prawns on top. Pour a spoonful of the dressing around the outside of the spinach leaves and serve.

Serving suggestions It is important to show off all the beautiful colours in this dish, and I would recommend that you use white plates to do this. Also make sure that there is a separation between the sauce around the outside and the green spinach leaves and prawns in the centre.

NATURALLY BALANCED Prawns are an excellent source of zinc. It has been suggested that a diet rich in this mineral may help prevent blindness associated with the ageing process. Research has also discovered that zinc is important for the maintenance of other senses such as taste and smell.

Rillette of avocado with tarragon and crème fraîche

This combination of rich avocado with the bitterness of tarragon is a refreshing way to start a dinner party. Rillette *is simply the French word for a coarse pâté.*

MAKES 4 PORTIONS

4 ripe avocados

Juice of 1 lemon

6 spring onions (scallions), finely chopped

100 ml/3½ fl oz/scant ½ cup crème fraîche or plain set Greek yoghurt

5 ml/1 tsp sea salt

Plenty of freshly ground black pepper

1 bunch of fresh tarragon

1 Cut the avocados in half, remove the stones (pits) and cut each piece in half. Peel off the skin (you should be able to do this easily if the fruit is ripe), chop the flesh into large dice and place in a large bowl.

2 Immediately add the lemon juice and stir round, then add the spring onions, crème fraîche or yoghurt, salt and pepper.

3 Remove the leaves from the tarragon by holding each sprig by the tip and running your fingers down the stem, stripping off the leaves. Coarsely chop the leaves and add them to the bowl.

4 Mix everything together using a fork, taking care to keep the texture of the avocado. Taste and adjust the seasoning if necessary.

5 Cover with clingfilm (plastic wrap) to prevent the mixture from turning brown.

Serving suggestions This coarse pâté goes very well with a Tomato and Chilli Salad (see page 27), and it is lovely served with my Marinated Prawn Cocktail (see page 113). You can also use the recipe to make a perfect canapé, served with ready-made miniature biscuits.

Hints and variations The rillette improves in flavour if made a few hours in advance. You can make it the night before, but do make sure it is well wrapped otherwise the avocado will turn dark on the surface. When an avocado is ripe, it should feel soft but not squashy. If you cannot buy tarragon, you can use chives instead.

NATURALLY BALANCED Avocado is naturally rich in lecithin – a great 'brain food' – and copper, which aids the formation of red blood cells. It is also believed to beautify the skin, so makes the perfect choice when you are trying to impress!

Fillets of smoked trout with a horseradish crust with watercress

The horseradish crust in this delicate starter helps to enhance the subtle flavour of the fish, while the bitter watercress salad is a perfect foil for the richness of the trout.

MAKES 4 PORTIONS

4 smoked trout fillets

¼ baguette, cut into small pieces

1 bunch of fresh flatleaf parsley, roughly chopped

20 ml/4 tsp creamed horseradish

1 bunch of fresh watercress

100 ml/3½ fl oz/scant ½ cup cold-pressed virgin olive oil

Juice of 1 lemon

Sea salt and freshly ground black pepper

1 Preheat the grill (broiler) to maximum.

2 Cut each trout fillet carefully in half diagonally and place on a baking (cookie) tray.

3 Place the bread, parsley and horseradish in a food processor or liquidiser and blend until the mixture breaks down into breadcrumbs and has turned a pale shade of green. Pat this mixture on top of each portion of fish so that the entire surface is covered with the bread topping. Place the tray in the fridge until required.

4 Put the watercress in a mixing bowl and toss with the olive oil, lemon juice and a little salt and pepper.

5 Just before you are ready to serve, place the tray of trout fillets under the grill, making sure the tray is not too close to the element of the grill. Grill (broil) for a few minutes until the topping begins to turn crisp and golden.

6 Place a small pile of watercress in the centre of each plate and drizzle the remaining sauce around the outside of the salad. Gently place two pieces of fish on top of the salad on each plate and serve immediately.

Serving suggestions This makes an excellent supper dish, accompanied by Roasted Sweet Potatoes (see page 85), with Sweet Tomato Dressing (see page 128) for the watercress salad.

Hints and variations You can prepare the topping and arrange it on the fish well in advance if you want to get this job out of the way; then keep the fish in the fridge until you are ready to flash them under the grill to crisp just before serving.

NATURALLY BALANCED Trout is an excellent source of the omega-3 fatty acid, linolenic acid, which it is thought may help to alleviate arthritis, migraines and heart disease.

Bourbon-marinated salmon with hazelnut oil

This dish is ideally suited as a starter for an evening meal as it is light and sophisticated but extremely easy to prepare. The alcohol in the bourbon actually cooks the salmon – and imparts a wonderful flavour at the same time. If you don't have bourbon, you can use Scotch whisky instead.

MAKES 4 PORTIONS

2 x 200 g/7 oz fresh salmon fillets, skinned and boned

A pinch of unrefined caster (superfine) sugar

Sea salt and freshly ground black pepper

6 spring onions (scallions), finely chopped

30 ml/2 tbsp bourbon

45 ml/3 tbsp good-quality hazelnut (filbert) oil

Juice of 1 lemon

15 ml/1 tbsp chopped fresh coriander (cilantro)

1 Place the salmon on a chopping board and use a sharp knife to slice the fish downwards as thinly as possible into fine strips.

2 Place the salmon strips in a shallow dish and season with a good pinch of sugar, some sea salt and freshly ground black pepper. Sprinkle over the spring onions, bourbon and hazelnut oil, cover and leave in the fridge to marinate for 30 minutes.

3 Remove from the fridge and tilt the dish to pour any juices into a bowl. Add the lemon juice and coriander to the bowl and mix together to make the dressing. Season to taste with salt and pepper.

4 Arrange the salmon slices on a large serving platter and drizzle the bourbon dressing over the top.

Serving suggestions I would accompany the fillets with salad leaves, lemon wedges and warm bread, all arranged separately. Serving it this way means that the focus is on the beautiful marinated salmon. If you prefer, you can combine the salad leaves and salmon on individual plates.

NATURALLY BALANCED Wild salmon is rapidly becoming an endangered species, although farmed salmon is readily available. Salmon is a good source of omega-3 essential fatty acids, which have a positive effect on the human brain, joints and skin. Unfortunately, there is much speculation about the growth hormones and dyes often used in farmed salmon feed, so it is best to buy your salmon from a recognised local source.

Chicken brochettes coated in peanut sauce

Brochette is simply the French word for 'kebab'. The distinctive feature of this recipe is the tangy garlic and lemon marinade, which complements and contrasts with the rich, sweet peanut sauce.

MAKES 4–6 PORTIONS

3 chicken breasts, skinned and boned

FOR THE MARINADE
30 ml/2 tbsp soy sauce

Grated zest and juice of 1 lemon

4 garlic cloves, finely crushed

FOR THE PEANUT SAUCE
225 g/8 oz/1 cup organic crunchy peanut butter

250 ml/8 fl oz/1 cup coconut milk

30 ml/2 tbsp clear honey

30 ml/2 tbsp soy sauce

5 ml/1 tsp dried chilli flakes

FOR GARNISH
A few sprigs of fresh coriander (cilantro)

1 lemon, cut into wedges

1 Slice the chicken into strips about 1 cm/½ in thick and place in a bowl. Mix together all the marinade ingredients, pour over the chicken and mix well. Leave to marinate for 20–30 minutes.

2 Meanwhile, purée all the peanut sauce ingredients in a food processor or liquidiser until smooth.

3 Preheat the grill (broiler) to maximum.

4 Thread the chicken on to skewers and place on a baking (cookie) tray. Grill (broil) for about 6 minutes, turning several times.

5 Brush the brochettes with a little of the peanut sauce, then continue to cook for a further 2–3 minutes until cooked through.

6 Heat the remaining sauce in a small pan or in the microwave.

7 Remove the brochettes from the grill and serve on a large platter, garnished with the coriander and lemon wedges. Serve the sauce in a separate bowl for dipping.

Serving suggestions These brochettes make an excellent starter to an impressive meal but if you are having a group of friends round for drinks, then serve tiny skewers as canapés on a single platter for people to help themselves. Do offer napkins to your guests in case anyone dribbles the peanut sauce!

Hints and variations You can thread almost anything on to a brochette skewer – from prawns (shrimp) to mushrooms, (bell) peppers to chunks of firm-fleshed fish. When you cook brochettes, soak the skewers in cold water for a few hours before you start, to prevent them from charring while the meat is cooking.

NATURALLY BALANCED Chicken is always popular with children and provides a low-fat alternative to red meat.

Risotto of leeks and lemon with pine nuts

If you have ever been lost for an idea on how to serve leeks, then try this dish – leeks with lemon are a wonderful, classic combination.

MAKES 6 PORTIONS

4–5 medium leeks

100 g/4 oz/1 cup pine kernels

100 g/4 oz/½ cup salted butter

Juice of 2 lemons

200 ml/7 fl oz/scant 1 cup white wine

Sea salt and
freshly ground black pepper

1 onion, finely chopped

500 g/18 oz/2¼ cups risotto rice

2 garlic cloves, crushed

1.2 litres/2 pts/5 cups
hot vegetable stock

1 bunch of fresh chives, finely snipped

1 Trim the leeks and cut them in half lengthways, leaving the root on while you clean them under cold, running water. (It makes it much easier if you leave the root intact.) Cut off the roots and slice the leeks, including the green parts, as finely as possible.

2 Place the pine kernels in a shallow pan and place on a high heat for about 4–5 minutes until lightly toasted, then remove them from the pan.

3 Melt half the butter in a large saucepan, add the leeks, half the lemon juice, half the wine and a good pinch of sea salt and pepper. Cover with a tight-fitting lid and cook on a medium-high heat for about 14 minutes until the leeks are tender.

4 While the leeks are cooking, heat the remaining butter in the risotto pan, add the chopped onion and sauté for 2 minutes, then add the rice and garlic and stir well until the rice is completely coated in onions and butter.

5 Add the remaining wine and simmer until the wine has reduced and the pan is almost dry.

6 Add a ladleful of stock to the pan, stirring continuously. Once the stock has been absorbed, add a little more stock, then continue in this way for about 14–16 minutes until the rice is tender but still just firm in the centre. You may need to add more stock and cook for longer, or you may be left with a little bit of stock, depending on the type of risotto rice you use.

7 Finish the risotto by stirring in the remaining lemon juice and season to taste with salt and pepper. Remove from the heat and add half the toasted pine nuts and half the snipped chives. Cover tightly and leave to stand.

8 Give the leeks a stir, then season to taste with salt and pepper.

9 Present the risotto in the centre of warmed plates, then gently place a small pile of leeks on top. Sprinkle each plate with the remaining chives and pine nuts and serve.

Serving suggestions If you prefer to allow the guests to help themselves, then spoon the risotto into a large warmed serving dish and sprinkle with the chives, and serve the leeks separately, sprinkled with the toasted pine nuts. This dish can be served on its own, but is particularly good with a mixed leaf salad, drizzled with olive oil and lemon juice.

Hints and variations The best risottos need lots of attention and stirring if you want to achieve a creamy and professional finish. The most commonly available risotto rice is arborio, but you will find other types in the supermarket; they all have a medium grain, which gives a creamy result. Allow a minimum of 75 g/3 oz/⅓ cup of medium-grain risotto rice per person. It is always best to cook risotto in a pan with low sides, such as a sauté pan or shallow saucepan.

NATURALLY BALANCED Pine kernels are full of vitamins and essential fatty acids and make a delicious snack on their own or as part of a lunch box.

Baked salmon with a rhubarb and ginger wine compôte

This is one of my favourite ways of serving salmon as it is light, refreshing and unusual. The rhubarb and ginger wine marry well with the richness of the salmon and help form an impressive dish, balanced in both texture and flavour.

MAKES 4 PORTIONS

4–6 medium sticks of rhubarb, finely chopped

1 lemon

25 g/1 oz/2 tbsp unrefined caster (superfine) sugar

200 ml/7 fl oz/scant 1 cup ginger wine

5 ml/1 tsp finely grated fresh root ginger

4 x 175 g/6 oz salmon fillets, skinned and boned

Sea salt and freshly ground black pepper

50 g/2 oz/¼ cup salted butter

A few sprigs of fresh flatleaf parsley

1 Preheat the oven to 200°C/400°F/gas 6/fan oven 180°C.

2 Put the rhubarb in a large saucepan. Cut the lemon in half. Cut one half into wedges and put aside. Squeeze the juice from the other half into the saucepan and add the sugar, half the ginger wine and the grated ginger. Bring to the boil, then reduce the heat and leave to simmer for 10 minutes until a little mushy.

3 Remove all the small bones from the salmon. Season the salmon fillets with salt and pepper and leave to one side.

4 Pour the rhubarb into a shallow ovenproof dish and lay the salmon fillets on top. Pour over the remaining ginger wine and lemon juice, then dot over with pieces of butter.

5 Bake in the preheated oven for about 20 minutes until the white protein starts to come to the surface or sides of the salmon.

6 Remove from the oven and gently lift the salmon fillets on to a plate to rest. Mix the rhubarb compôte well with a fork, then put a good spoonful on to the centre of each serving plate. Place a fillet of salmon on each portion of rhubarb and garnish with a sprig of flatleaf parsley and a wedge of lemon.

Serving suggestions This dish is perfect with plain new potatoes and a simple green vegetable. A small glass of ginger wine with a few ice cubes added makes a delicious refreshing drink to accompany it.

Hints and variations This rhubarb and ginger wine compôte also works very well with chicken breasts. Chicken takes longer to cook than salmon, so increase the cooking time to 25 minutes in the oven and make sure the chicken is cooked through before serving.

**Photograph opposite:
Mango and Papaya Cocktail with
Coconut Liqueur (see page 131).**

FOOD TO IMPRESS

Warm duck salad with crispy skin and peaches

If you usually find duck too fatty, then try serving it this way. The duck skin is cooked separately from the duck breast and becomes beautifully crisp once cooked. This duck salad makes an impressive starter or a special light lunch.
See photograph opposite page 97.

**MAKES 4 STARTER PORTIONS OR
2 MAIN COURSE PORTIONS**

2 large duck breasts

**Sea salt and
freshly ground black pepper**

200 g/7 oz cherry tomatoes, cut in half

30 ml/2 tbsp walnut oil

Juice of ½ lemon

225 g/8 oz mixed salad leaves

**1 ripe peach, peeled, stoned (pitted)
and thinly sliced**

1 Preheat the grill (broiler) to maximum.

2 Using a sharp knife, remove the skin from the duck breasts. Slice the skin into fine strips and season with a pinch of sea salt.

3 Place the skin in a medium frying pan (skillet) set on a high heat and cook for 10–12 minutes until crisp.

4 Season the duck breast generously with salt and pepper and place on a baking (cookie) tray under the grill. Cook for about 4 minutes on each side until done to your liking.

5 Toss the tomatoes, walnut oil and lemon juice with the salad leaves.

6 Remove the cooked duck from the grill and leave to rest. Cut off the crispy skin and strain off the fat. Slice the duck very thinly.

7 Place a small mound of salad on each plate and arrange the duck slices on it. Garnish with the duck skin and slices of peach.

Serving suggestions To make this a more substantial dish, use the duck fat to sauté some cooked new potatoes with a little crushed garlic and serve with the warm duck salad.

Hints and variations Barbary duck is one of the most common types reared in the UK, while Rouen is the type usually eaten in France. The latter are extremely tasty but tend to be very fatty.

NATURALLY BALANCED Although duck fat is natural and therefore the body can break it down, it is a saturated fat and should only be eaten sparingly, otherwise it can contribute to high blood pressure.

FOOD TO IMPRESS

**Photograph opposite:
Apple and Apricot Compôte in
Crispy Filo Baskets (see page 135).**

Venison steaks with orange, prunes and cinnamon

Venison is an extremely lean and nutritious red meat, which has retained a certain sense of sophistication despite being now quite affordable and widely available. This recipe makes a great use of the classic combination of prunes and oranges, with freshly grated cinnamon and crushed juniper berries providing added zest.

MAKES 4 PORTIONS

10 stoned (pitted) prunes

200 ml/7 fl oz/scant 1 cup kettle-hot water

2 large oranges

4 x 175 g/6 oz venison steaks

8 juniper berries, coarsely crushed

½ cinnamon stick, finely grated

Sea salt and freshly ground black pepper

30 ml/2 tbsp sunflower oil

50 g/2 oz/¼ cup salted butter

100 ml/3½ fl oz/scant 1 cup port

1 Put the prunes and hot water in a bowl and leave to soak. Grate the zest from one of the oranges and squeeze the juice from both.

2 Season the venison with the orange zest, juniper berries, cinnamon, salt and pepper.

3 Heat a medium-sized frying pan (skillet) or sauté pan. Add the sunflower oil and heat, then add the venison steaks and cook for 2 minutes. Add half the butter to the pan, then turn over the steaks and cook the other side for 2 minutes. Don't add the butter earlier, or it may burn.

4 While the steaks are cooking, coarsely chop the prunes, reserving any juice, then mix with the orange juice.

5 Once the venison has finished cooking, remove from the pan and leave to rest on a plate. Add the prunes, orange juice and port to the pan and scrape the base of the pan to remove any sediment. Once the port comes to the boil, whisk in the remaining butter, then strain the sauce through a fine sieve (strainer).

6 Place the venison steaks on a warmed serving platter and drizzle the prune and orange sauce over top.

Serving suggestions This tastes wonderful with my Simple Creamy Mashed Potatoes (see page 101) and minted peas.

Hints and variations This combination of juniper, orange and cinnamon also goes very well with duck breasts, which can be cooked using the same method.

NATURALLY BALANCED Although the body is perfectly capable of breaking down and utilising natural saturated fat, in general we consume more fat in our Western diet than we need for energy. It is therefore much more healthy to avoid saturated fats, reduce our intake of meat, and eat only lean meat with any excess fat trimmed off.

Crispy chicken thins with garlic butter

An extremely light main course, this makes great use of the delicious taste of good-quality chicken. I recommend that you buy organic chicken breasts – they are a little more expensive but this dish requires only a small quantity of meat per person. You'll taste the difference, and be happier knowing that the chicken was raised humanely.

MAKES 4 PORTIONS

2 x 200 g/7 oz chicken breasts

A generous pinch of paprika

Sea salt and freshly ground black pepper

15 ml/1 tbsp unbleached plain (all-purpose) flour

1 large free-range egg, beaten

15 ml/1 tbsp milk

100 g/4 oz/1 cup fine dried breadcrumbs

100 g/4 oz/½ cup salted butter

3 lemons

2 garlic cloves, crushed

15 ml/1 tbsp chopped fresh parsley

1 Slice each chicken breast in half horizontally and lay flat on a chopping board, then carefully slice horizontally again, to give eight pieces. Cover with clingfilm (plastic wrap) and bat out with either a rolling pin or meat tenderiser until very thin.

2 Season each piece of chicken on both sides with paprika, salt and pepper, then dust with flour.

3 Mix the beaten egg with the milk and spread the breadcrumbs on a tray. Dip each piece of chicken quickly into the egg mixture, then on to the tray of breadcrumbs, until well coated.

4 Heat a large frying pan (skillet) and add the half of the butter. When the butter begins to sizzle, place four of the chicken pieces in the pan and cook for just 2 minutes on each side. Be careful not to allow the pan to get too hot or the butter may burn.

5 Once the chicken pieces are cooked, remove from the pan and leave to rest on a plate. Add the remaining butter to the pan, cook the other four slices, then transfer them to the plate.

6 Squeeze the juice from one lemon and cut the other two in half. Add the lemon juice and garlic to the pan and stir well. Add the chopped parsley and stir again, then pour the mixture over the chicken.

7 Serve the chicken slices with the lemon halves on the side.

Serving suggestions I would suggest a side dish of Simple Creamy Mashed Potatoes (see page 101) with these crispy chicken wafers, or perhaps Broccoli and Almond Mash (see page 102).

NATURALLY BALANCED I prefer to choose organic chicken and avoid commercial battery-raised birds. These poor creatures are fed food laden with chemicals, hormones and antibiotics and many food scientists believe that this is then passed down through the food chain.

Caramelised onion sauce

Onions, red wine and a well-flavoured stock are the three ingredients that make this a truly delicious, rich sauce.

MAKES 4–6 PORTIONS

15 ml/1 tbsp sunflower oil

3 onions, thinly sliced

25 g/1 oz/2 tbsp salted butter

2 garlic cloves, crushed

200 ml/7 fl oz/scant 1 cup red wine

500 ml/17 fl oz/2¼ cups vegetable stock

Juice of ¼ lemon

5 ml/1 tsp cornflour (cornstarch) or potato flour

Sea salt and freshly ground black pepper

1 Heat a shallow saucepan or sauté pan and add the oil. When the oil is hot, add the onions and brown them gently for 3–4 minutes. Then, add the butter and garlic and sauté for a further 2–3 minutes.

2 Add the wine, bring to the boil and allow the wine to reduce by about half. Add the stock and lemon juice and bring to the boil again.

3 Mix the cornflour or potato flour with a little cold water, then stir in a ladleful of the sauce. Whisk until smooth, then pour into the saucepan and whisk well. Heat the sauce to thicken slightly and cook gently for a further 5 minutes.

4 Season to taste with a little salt and pepper before serving.

Serving suggestion This sauce will complement almost any roasted and grilled (broiled) meat dishes. It is also excellent with my Cashew and Quinoa Cheese Loaf (see page 69).

Citrus and ginger dressing

MAKES 4–6 PORTIONS

1 pink grapefruit

1 orange

1 lemon

60 ml/4 tbsp cold-pressed virgin olive oil

45 ml/3 tbsp light soy sauce

5 ml/1 tsp finely grated fresh root ginger or 2.5 ml/½ tsp ground ginger

A pinch of ground coriander (cilantro)

15 ml/1 tbsp chopped fresh coriander

1 Remove the peel and white pith from the citrus fruits then, using a small sharp or serrated knife, cut the segments of fruit out into a bowl. Pick out any pips and reserve any juice in the same bowl.

2 Add the oil, soy sauce, spices and fresh coriander and mix all the ingredients together. Stand for 5 minutes to allow the flavours to develop, before using.

Serving suggestions An extremely refreshing dressing, this can be served with all types of dishes, warm or cold. I like it with plain grilled (broiled) salmon or roasted vegetables with feta cheese.

Hints and variations If you wish, you can gently warm the dressing but do not overheat it or the citrus fruit segments will break down and lose their individual characteristics.

Flavoured butters

Flavoured butters are simplicity itself to make. Each one of the recipes here makes a roll of butter that you can simply store in your fridge or freezer, ready for use.

MAKES 1 x 12 CM/5 IN ROLL

250 g/2 oz/¼ cup salted butter, softened

**Sea salt and
freshly ground black pepper**

**FOR GARLIC AND ALMOND BUTTER
WITH TARRAGON**

50 g/2 oz/½ cup ground almonds

4 garlic cloves, crushed

1 large free-range egg yolk

15 ml/1 tbsp chopped fresh tarragon

10 ml/2 tsp Worcestershire sauce

Juice of ½ lemon

FOR CHILLI AND LIME BUTTER

3 red chillis, seeded and finely chopped

Grated zest and juice of 1 lime

5 ml/1 tsp chilli powder

**A pinch of unrefined caster
(superfine) sugar**

FOR OLIVE AND ROSEMARY BUTTER

**10 black olives, stoned (pitted) and
finely chopped**

30 ml/2 tbsp cold-pressed virgin olive oil

5 ml/1 tsp dried rosemary

1 Make sure the butter is soft.

2 Gradually work the butter into all the listed ingredients for the flavour you want to make and season to taste with a little salt and pepper.

3 Form the flavoured butter into a sausage shape and lay on a sheet of clingfilm (plastic wrap) or foil. Roll up and tie into a neat roll of butter. Chill until ready to serve.

Serving suggestions Put a slice of butter on boiled new potatoes or other vegetables, use to spread on warm bread, or dot on to meat or fish to be grilled (broiled) to give it extra flavour.

Hints and variations You can keep the butter in the freezer for up to a month and you can slice off whatever you need, using a serrated knife, without defrosting the whole roll.

Use this method to make any type of butter you like, varying the ingredients according to season and your own favourite ingredients.

NATURALLY BALANCED One argument for choosing organic butter is that other commercially made butters can contain growth hormones and antibiotics that have found their way into the butter through the animal from its feed. As butter is such a concentrated dairy food, this is another good reason not to use too much butter in your diet.

Teriyaki sauce

This makes a deliciously sticky sweet and salty sauce. The flavour is very powerful, so you only need a small quantity per person.

MAKES 6–8 PORTIONS

90 ml/6 tbsp soy sauce

45 ml/3 tbsp soft brown sugar

45 ml/3 tbsp dry sherry

5 ml/1 tsp cornflour (cornstarch)

15 ml/1 tbsp cold water

1 Put the soy sauce, sugar and sherry in a small saucepan and bring to the boil, being careful not to allow the sauce to boil over.

2 Mix the cornflour and water to a paste, then whisk a little of the hot mixture into it. Pour the cornflour mixture into the sauce and bring back to the boil, whisking occasionally until the sauce thickens.

Serving suggestions Spread over grilled (broiled) or barbecued steaks or add a little to your stir-fries.

NATURALLY BALANCED Modern-day manufacturing of soy sauce uses wheat, instead of soya beans. If you cannot tolerate wheat, you need to use a product called tamari, which is brewed from soya beans.

Lemon and lime dressing

This sauce has a wonderful bright, vibrant colour.

MAKES 6 PORTIONS

Juice of 1 lime

Juice of 1 lemon

15 ml/1 tbsp sherry vinegar

1 garlic clove, finely crushed

10 ml/2 tsp clear honey

2.5 ml/½ tsp ground cumin

2.5 ml/½ tsp ground cardamom

A pinch of sea salt

90 ml/6 tbsp cold-pressed virgin olive oil

30 ml/2 tbsp chopped fresh coriander (cilantro)

1 Whisk together all the ingredients except the oil and fresh coriander.

2 Gradually pour in the oil, whisking all the time.

3 Taste and adjust the seasoning and add the chopped coriander just before serving.

Serving suggestions This dressing should be served cold with light dishes such as my Crispy Chicken Thins (see page 123) and Risotto of Leeks (see page 118).

Hints and variations The dressing will begin to turn brown once the coriander is added, so if you intend to store it, stop after step 2. The sauce will keep well like this in the fridge for at least a month.

NATURALLY BALANCED Try making salad dressings with flaxseed or hemp oil for something different – both are available in health food stores.

Simple salad dressing

This is a classic dressing, suitable for everyday use.

MAKES 6–8 PORTIONS

15 ml/1 tbsp clear honey

30 ml/2 tbsp white wine vinegar

15 ml/1 tbsp Dijon mustard

15 ml/1 tbsp finely chopped shallots

Cayenne

A pinch of sea salt

100 ml/3½ fl oz/scant ½ cup
cold-pressed virgin olive oil

100 ml/3½ fl oz/scant ½ cup
sunflower oil

1 Put add all the ingredients except the oils in a large mixing bowl, adjusting the cayenne and salt to taste, and whisk together well.

2 Gradually add the oils, whisking all the time. If the dressing thickens too much, trickle in 15 ml/1 tbsp of hot water, still continuing to whisk.

3 Check the seasoning before serving.

Hints and variations This dressing does not separate when chilled, and will keep in the fridge for at least a month. If you make it in bulk you will find a food processor or liquidiser very helpful.

You can vary the dressing by adding other ingredients, such as poppy seeds, a touch of soy sauce or even a little citrus juice.

NATURALLY BALANCED It is important to use the best-quality oils in your cooking. Cold-pressed oil means that the seeds have not been heat-treated in order to extract the oil, and it has a clean and pleasant taste. Once the source ingredients are heat-treated, it can make the oil harmful.

Sweet tomato dressing

This dressing is vibrant and naturally balanced in its sweet and sour taste. The olive oil brings out the mustard flavour, which in turn enhances the taste of the tomato.

MAKES 6–8 PORTIONS

4 very ripe tomatoes, chopped

5 ml/1 tsp wholegrain mustard

5 ml/1 tsp Dijon mustard

15 ml/1 tbsp white wine vinegar

15 ml/1 tbsp kettle-hot water

15 ml/1 tbsp unrefined caster (superfine) sugar

10 ml/2 tsp tomato purée (paste)

60 ml/4 tbsp cold-pressed virgin olive oil

Sea salt and freshly ground black pepper

1 Put all the ingredients except the oil and seasoning into a liquidiser or food processor and start to blend.

2 Gradually trickle in the oil, with the motor running, until the dressing thickens and emulsifies. As soon as it is thick enough, stop adding the oil. If it thickens too much, add a little more hot water.

3 To remove the tomato seeds, rub the contents through a sieve (strainer).

4 Season with salt and pepper and taste the dressing. If it's a little sour, add a little more sugar; if it's too sweet, add a dash of vinegar.

Serving suggestions This dressing can be drizzled over any chicken or fish. You can also use it as a salad dressing or even toss with wholemeal pasta for a delicious pasta salad.

Hints and variations This dressing will keep in the fridge for four or five days.

NATURALLY BALANCED It is always best to look for cold-pressed virgin olive oil packaged in dark glass, which helps to protect it from sunlight.

Chocolate truff with raspberries and framboise liqueur

The contrast between the richness of the chocolate and the sharpness of the raspberries is simply delicious. Choose chocolate with at least 70 per cent cocoa solids for that wonderful bitter, strong flavour. You do need to make this at least four hours in advance to give the chocolate time to set.

MAKES 6 PORTIONS

1 Foolproof Chocolate Cake (see page 60)

300 g/11 oz fresh raspberries

60 ml/4 tbsp framboise liqueur

250 g/9 oz good-quality plain (semi-sweet) chocolate

375 ml/13 fl oz/1½ cups double (heavy) cream

25 g/1 oz/2 tbsp icing (confectioners') sugar, sifted

1 Lightly brush the inside of a 450 g/1 lb loaf tin (pan) with water, then gently press a layer of clingfilm (plastic wrap) to line the inside.

2 Slice the chocolate cake horizontally so that you get a long slice about 1 cm/½ in thick. Lay this in the bottom of the tin and scatter over the raspberries. Drizzle with 30 ml/2 tbsp of the liqueur. The remainder of the cake can be frozen for future use.

3 Melt the chocolate in a heatproof bowl set over a pan of gently simmering water. Do not overheat, otherwise it will go grainy. As soon as it has melted, remove it from the heat and leave to cool.

4 Whip the cream in a large bowl until it forms soft peaks, then add the icing sugar and the remaining liqueur. Whisk again until just firm

5 Gently fold the chocolate into the cream. Work fairly quickly otherwise the chocolate will set slightly, leaving tiny flecks. Pour into the tin and smooth the top with a palette knife. Wrap with clingfilm and chill in the fridge for at least 4 hours.

6 To serve, turn the truff out of the tin, remove the clingfilm and slice with a warm knife.

Serving suggestion Serve each slice on a plate, dusted with icing sugar. Add a few fresh raspberries and drizzle with more liqueur.

Hints and variations You can use frozen raspberries if fresh are not available. The dessert may also be frozen although you will lose the texture.

NATURALLY BALANCED Chocolate is often made using a high percentage of vegetable oil and sugar. Really good-quality chocolate, made with over 70 per cent cocoa solids, retains more of the nutritious elements of the cocoa.

Lemon and lime curd with passion fruit

An extremely refreshing dessert but still beautifully rich, the texture of this curd is similar to that of a crème brûlée. The curd is best made at least 4 hours in advance, or even the day before, to allow time for it to set and for the flavours of lemon and lime to blend and mature.

MAKES 4–6 PORTIONS

3 large lemons

4 limes

6 large free-range whole eggs

6 large free-range egg yolks

175 g/6 oz/¾ cup unrefined caster (superfine) sugar

150 g/5 oz/⅔ cup unsalted (sweet) butter, diced

3 passion fruit

1 Grate the zest from one of the lemons and one of the limes. Squeeze the juice from all the citrus fruit.

2 Place the lemon and lime juices and zest, the eggs, egg yolks and sugar in a large heatproof bowl. Set over a saucepan half-filled with gently simmering water and heat gently for at least 30 minutes, whisking around the edges every 5–6 minutes, until the mixture thickens to a thick custard consistency.

3 Remove from the heat and rub through a fine sieve (strainer) into a clean bowl, then stir in the diced butter and whisk to incorporate well.

4 Pour into individual dishes, such as ramekins (custard cups).

5 Halve the passion fruit, then scoop out the flesh and spread over the top of the cups of curd.

6 Leave to cool, then chill in the fridge for about 1 hour until set.

Hints and variations You can easily turn this dessert into a brûlée. Simply sprinkle with sugar and caramelise with a blowtorch or place under a preheated hot grill (broiler).

NATURALLY BALANCED It is always advisable to wash and scrub citrus fruits before you grate them as they are often covered in wax. There is no evidence to suggest that the wax on fruit is harmful to the body, but it certainly is indigestible. Fortunately, many supermarkets now sell the unwaxed varieties.

FOOD TO IMPRESS

Mango and papaya cocktail with coconut liqueur

To finish your impressive meal with something exotic and refreshing, try this fruit salad – it has a real zing of lime and mint. You can use other fruits, but I think mango and papaya are perfect.

See photograph opposite page 120.

MAKES 4 PORTIONS

100 ml/3½ fl oz/scant ½ cup coconut liqueur

Grated zest and juice of 1 lime

2 ripe papayas (pawpaw)

2 ripe mangoes

100 g/4 oz strawberries

1 Whisk together the coconut liqueur and lime zest and juice.

2 Peel, stone (pit) and dice or slice the papayas and mangoes and hull the strawberries.

3 Mix the fruit with the marinade and leave in the fridge for 30 minutes to chill.

4 Serve in wine or cocktail glasses.

Serving suggestions This dessert is delicious with fruit-flavoured ice creams and sorbets, or you could try serving it with my Ginger and Honey Tuille Biscuits (see page 63).

NATURALLY BALANCED We should all be eating more fruit. It is an essential part of a healthy balanced diet, is full of vitamins and other nutrients – and is so delicious, especially now we have such a wide choice available in supermarkets. If you needed any more reasons, fruit is also believed to be an excellent remedy for stress!

Lime-marinated strawberries with fresh mint

Although you can now buy strawberries all the year round, I think it is best to buy local fruit in season – or even pick your own – to get the very best flavour. The sharpness of the lime in this recipe counterbalances the sweetness of the strawberries to give a truly wonderful flavour.

MAKES 4–6 PORTIONS

100 g/4 oz/½ cup unrefined caster (superfine) sugar

100 ml/3½ fl oz/scant ½ cup water

Grated zest and juice of 2 limes

400 g/14 oz strawberries, hulled and halved, if large

15 ml/1 tbsp finely chopped fresh mint

1 Put the sugar and water in a saucepan and bring to the boil. Reduce the heat and simmer for 1–2 minutes to form a syrup. Remove from the heat, stir in the lime zest and pour into a bowl. Leave to cool slightly.

2 Stir in the lime juice.

3 Add the strawberries to the syrup and place in the fridge to chill for 3–4 hours.

4 Just before serving, stir in the chopped fresh mint.

Serving suggestions This dessert is delicious served cold with just a dollop of crème fraîche or plain Greek yoghurt.

NATURALLY BALANCED Strawberries are believed to be excellent for the digestion, so make the perfect end to a meal. They are also supposed to be an aphrodisiac, so be careful who you are trying to impress!

Whisky and honey ice cream with candied lemons

*You don't need an ice cream maker to make delicious ice cream with this recipe –
the alcohol prevents crystals forming, so there is no need for constant churning.*

MAKES 4–6 PORTIONS

300 ml/½ pt/1¼ cups double (heavy)
cream

60 ml/4 tbsp Scotch whisky

45 ml/3 tbsp clear honey

4 large free-range egg yolks

1 lemon

125 g/4½ oz/generous ½ cup unrefined
caster (superfine) sugar

50 ml/2 fl oz/3½ tbsp water

1 Whisk the cream until thick, then gradually whisk in the whisky.

2 Heat the honey gently in a pan or in the microwave just to warm it; don't allow it to boil.

3 Whisk the egg yolks in a bowl, then slowly pour in the honey, whisking continuously (use an electric whisk if you have one), until the mixture is pale and thick.

4 Gently fold in the thick whisky-flavoured cream.

5 Pour into a freezer container and freeze until firm. This will take about 3–4 hours.

6 Cut the lemon in half and remove any pips. Slice the lemon as thinly as possible, then place in a pan and add just enough water to cover. Bring to the boil, then reduce the heat and simmer for 5 minutes. Drain off the water and return the lemon slices to the same pan.

7 Add the sugar and measured water and bring to the boil again, then simmer for 10 minutes until the syrup is transparent. Turn off the heat and leave the lemon slices to cool in the syrup.

8 Serve the whisky ice cream in little dishes with slices of candied lemon on top.

Serving suggestions To make this a really impressive dessert, you could create individual baskets with my Ginger and Honey Tuille Biscuits (see page 63) and present the ice cream in those, with the candied lemon slices on top.

NATURALLY BALANCED Honey makes an excellent sweetener in drinks and desserts. It is much sweeter than sugar and so you need only about half the quantity.

Roasted pineapple with chilli and ginger

An amazing chemical reaction happens between pineapple and chilli as they cook together: the chilli brings out the sweetness of the pineapple and the pineapple takes the heat out of the chilli. Vanilla pods cost a little more than essence (extract), but they do add an exotic finishing touch to this unusual dessert.

MAKES 4–6 PORTIONS

125 g/4½ oz/generous ½ cup unrefined caster (superfine) sugar, plus a little extra

1 ripe pineapple

2 vanilla pods

1 red chilli, seeded

1 cm/½ in piece of fresh root ginger, peeled

100 ml/3½ fl oz/scant ½ cup crème fraîche

1 ripe banana, mashed

15 ml/1 tbsp dark rum

1 Preheat the oven to 200°C/400°F/gas 6/fan oven 180°C.

2 Put the measured sugar and 15 ml/1 tbsp water in a small saucepan and heat gently until the sugar has melted. Bring to the boil, then boil without stirring for at least 4–5 minutes until the sugar turns to a light caramel colour.

3 Meanwhile, peel the pineapple, cut into 1 cm/½ in rounds and place in a baking dish. Split the vanilla pods in half lengthways, then break each half into two pieces. Scrape out the seeds, but don't throw them away. Chop the chilli with a little extra sugar.

4 Add 100 ml/3½ fl oz/scant ½ cup cold water to the caramelised sugar, then stir in the pieces of vanilla pod and the seeds, the chilli, ginger, crème fraîche, banana and rum. Pour over the pineapple.

5 Bake in the preheated oven for 30 minutes, spooning the sauce over the pineapple occasionally.

6 Place the pineapple slices on a plate with the sauce poured over. Top each slice with a strip of vanilla pod and serve warm.

Serving suggestions This impressive pineapple dessert needs only some ice cream or extra crème fraîche on the side.

NATURALLY BALANCED Pineapple is a natural source of the enzyme bromelin, which is known to be an aid to digestion and also an anti-inflammatory, suggesting that it may be good for the joints in particular.

Apple and apricot compôte in crispy filo baskets

This dessert is a unique way to end a dinner party. Warming and spiced with mace, the apple and apricot compôte marries well with the walnut yoghurt, and the filo cases add texture to the dish.

See photograph opposite page 121.

MAKES 4 PORTIONS

A little sunflower oil, for greasing

75 g/3 oz/½ cup dried unsulphured apricots

4 sheets of filo pastry (paste)

50 g/2 oz/¼ cup unsalted (sweet) butter, softened

500 g/18 oz apples, peeled, cored and chopped

25 g/1 oz/2 tbsp demerara sugar

2.5 ml/½ tsp ground mace

2.5 ml/½ tsp ground cinnamon

Juice of 1 lemon

50 g/2 oz/½ cup walnut halves, crushed

200 ml/7 fl oz/scant 1 cup plain set Greek yoghurt

15 ml/1 tbsp maple syrup

1 Preheat the oven to 200°C/400°F/gas 6/fan oven 180°C. Grease four ramekin dishes (custard cups) with sunflower oil.

2 Soak the apricots in a little hot water while you prepare the filo cases.

3 Lay two sheets of filo pastry on a clean surface and brush very lightly with the softened butter. Place another sheet on top of each, then cut in half so that you have four rectangular sheets of pastry.

4 Lay the sheets in the ramekins, pressing them gently against the sides and allowing the pastry at the top to stick up above the ramekin slightly. Place on a baking (cookie) tray and cook in the preheated oven for 8–9 minutes until golden. Remove from the oven.

5 Melt the remaining butter in a saucepan and sauté the apples, sugar, ground mace and cinnamon for a few minutes.

6 Drain and finely chop the apricots and add to the compôte with the lemon juice. Turn down the heat, cover and simmer for 10 minutes.

7 Mix the walnuts with the yoghurt and half the maple syrup.

8 Place the filo 'baskets' on plates and fill with the compôte. Spoon some walnut yoghurt on the side and drizzle with maple syrup.

Serving suggestions Place a little of the compôte on the plate first, then sit the crispy cups on it so that they lean slightly forward. Fill with compôte so that it is cascading out of the pastry shell.

Hints and variations You can make the compôte with any fruit of your choice.

NATURALLY BALANCED Apples and apricots are both high in complex carbohydrates, which help to maintain a steady level of glucose in the bloodstream and provide the energy and nutrients the body needs.

Banana ice cream with pecan and maple syrup

A very simple and delicious ice cream to finish a special meal, this mixture does not require an ice cream maker and has a lovely smooth and velvety texture. This recipe uses the classic American combination of pecan nuts and maple syrup.

MAKES 4 PORTIONS

5 very ripe bananas

250 ml/8 fl oz/1 cup double (heavy) cream

400 ml/14 fl oz/1¾ cups fresh orange juice

30 ml/2 tbsp maple syrup

100 g/4 oz/1 cup pecan halves

1 Peel and mash the bananas in a large bowl. Mix in the cream, orange juice, and 15 ml/1 tbsp of the maple syrup.

2 Crush the pecans with the side of a cook's knife or in a pestle and mortar and add half to the mixture.

3 Pour into a freezer container and place in the freezer overnight.

4 Scoop into individual bowls with the remaining pecans sprinkled on top and drizzle with the remaining maple syrup.

Serving suggestions As this is such a simple dessert, you could spend a little extra time making some baskets in which to serve the ice cream. Use the recipe for Ginger and Honey Tuille Biscuits (see page 63) or Crispy Filo Baskets (see page 135).

NATURALLY BALANCED There is some evidence that bananas may actually improve the quality of your sleep. This is because they help to stimulate the production of seratonin, the hormone that affects our moods. What a good excuse to eat a bowl of this ice cream before you go to bed – but make sure you brush your teeth afterwards!

Fresh figs with mascarpone and pistachios

This is a very different dessert – and perfect for those who like to finish a meal with a sweet as well as those who like cheese. Mascarpone, an Italian cream cheese, is very rich, so I like to combine it with an equal quantity of plain Greek yoghurt.

MAKES 4 PORTIONS

12 fresh figs

30 ml/2 tbsp clear honey

100 g/4 oz/½ cup mascarpone cheese

100 ml/4 fl oz/½ cup plain Greek yoghurt

10 ml/2 tsp finely chopped fresh mint

100 g/4 oz/1 cup unsalted pistachios, crushed

1 Preheat the grill (broiler) to maximum.

2 Wipe the figs with a damp cloth, then cut a deep cross in the top of each of them using a serrated knife. Take care not to damage them as they are quite delicate.

3 Place on a baking (cookie) tray and drizzle with half of the honey. Place under the grill for 2–3 minutes.

4 Mix together the mascarpone and yoghurt with the remaining honey and the fresh mint.

5 Remove the figs from the grill and place three in each of four individual dishes. Carefully place a spoonful of the yoghurt mixture into the middle of each one, then sprinkle with the pistachios. Drizzle over a little more honey, if desired.

Hints and variations You can serve the figs fresh, without even grilling them, if you like. You can also try using ricotta cheese if you find mascarpone too rich.

NATURALLY BALANCED Figs are one of the most alkalising foods and help balance acidic conditions that result from a diet rich in meat and refined foods. They are also an excellent cure for constipation because of their gentle laxative properties.

Mango and lime pavlova roll

This is another of my grandma's recipes and it's delicious. You need to use canned mango rather than fresh, as the acid in fresh mangoes will react with the cream filling and deflate it – as I found out the first time I tried it!

MAKES 4–6 PORTIONS

3 large free-range egg whites

A pinch of sea salt

250 g/9 oz/generous 1 cup unrefined caster (superfine) sugar

15 ml/1 tbsp cornflour (cornstarch)

7.5 ml/1½ tsp white wine vinegar

2.5 ml/½ tsp vanilla essence (extract)

Grated zest and juice of 1 lime

1 x 425 g/14 oz/large can of mango slices, drained and roughly chopped

300 ml/½ pt/1¼ cups double (heavy) cream

A little icing (confectioners') sugar

1 Preheat the oven to 150°C/300°F/gas 2/fan oven 135°C and line a Swiss roll tin (jelly roll pan) with non-stick baking parchment.

2 Beat the egg whites and salt until stiff.

3 Add 175 g/6 oz/¾ cup of the sugar a tablespoon at a time, whisking each addition until stiff and glossy.

4 Beat in the cornflour, vinegar and vanilla essence.

5 Using a palette knife, spread the meringue into the lined tin and bake in the preheated oven for 30 minutes.

6 Remove from the oven, turn out the roulade on to a clean sheet of greaseproof (waxed) paper, lay a second sheet on top, and whilst still warm, roll up gently and loosely.

7 Stir the lime zest and juice into the mango with the remaining sugar.

8 Whisk the cream until softly peaking, then fold into the mango mixture. Chill until slightly firm.

9 Carefully unroll the roulade and spread the mango mixture over the surface, leaving about 2.5 cm/5 in around the edges. Gently roll up again, then wrap in the paper and clingfilm (plastic wrap) to help it keep its shape. Freeze until firm, then dust with icing sugar just before serving.

Serving suggestions The sharpness of Lime-marinated Strawberries (see page 132) will marry perfectly with the sweetness of the Mango and Lime Pavlova Roll.

NATURALLY BALANCED Always add a little lime juice to mango – it helps draw the sweetness from the fruit, which in turn balances the acidity of the lime.

FOOD TO IMPRESS

Poached vanilla pears with a sweet hazelnut risotto

Although serving risotto for dessert may sound a little odd, if you make this recipe with love and attention – and plenty of steam and stirring as you add the stock – then it will be a dessert to remember.

MAKE 4 PORTIONS

50 g/2 oz/⅓ cup dried unsulphured apricots

1 vanilla pod

450 ml/¾ pt/2 cups water

100 g/4 oz/½ cup unrefined caster (superfine) sugar

Grated zest of ½ lemon

4 cardamom pods, crushed

4 small firm pears such as Comice

25 g/1 oz/2 tbsp unsalted (sweet) butter

25 g/1 oz/¼ cup hazelnuts (filberts)

100 g/4 oz/½ cup medium-grain risotto rice

100 ml/3½ fl oz/scant ½ cup plain set Greek yoghurt

1 Soak the apricots in a bowl of boiling water.

2 Split open the vanilla pod, scrape out the seeds and reserve them.

3 Place the pod with the measured water, sugar, lemon zest and cardamom pods in a small saucepan and bring to the boil, then turn down the heat and leave to simmer gently.

4 Peel and trim the pears and place in the syrup. Poach for 10–12 minutes until tender. Remove the pears from the pan. Strain the syrup through a sieve (strainer) and reserve 400 ml/14 fl oz/ 1¾ cups of the liquid – you will need it to make the risotto. Using a small sharp knife, cut five little slits in each pear, starting about 2.5 cm/1 in from the top and going down to the bottom.

5 Drain the apricots, reserving any soaking liquid, and chop the fruit.

6 Put a sauté pan or shallow saucepan over a high heat and add the butter. When it has melted, add the hazelnuts and rice and sauté for 1–2 minutes until all the ingredients are coated in butter.

7 Add the apricots and their soaking liquid with a ladleful of the pear stock and stir well until the liquid has been absorbed by the rice. Keep adding the stock a ladleful at a time until all the liquid has been absorbed and the rice is creamy and tender. This should take about 10 minutes. If the rice is still a little chewy when you have added all the liquid, then add a little milk or water and continue to cook.

8 Remove from the heat, remove the vanilla pod and stir in the yoghurt and vanilla seeds.

9 Serve a little mound of risotto on each plate, then sit a poached pear next to the risotto and press down so that it fans out slightly.

Serving suggestions You can serve this risotto with other desserts such as Fresh Figs with Mascarpone and Pistachios (see page 137).

Rhubarb and orange fruit fool with ginger

This is such a delicious way to finish a meal – ginger and orange complement the rhubarb beautifully and fruit fool is so light and refreshing, there is always room for it, even after a heavy main course. It is the perfect make-ahead dinner-party dessert as it can easily be made the day before and left overnight in the fridge.

MAKES 4–6 PORTIONS

450 g/1 lb rhubarb, peeled if thick

225 g/8 oz/1 cup unrefined caster (superfine) sugar

Grated zest and juice of ½ orange

2.5 cm/1 in piece of fresh root ginger, peeled and grated

5 ml/1 tsp ground ginger

2.5 ml/½ tsp vanilla essence (extract)

250 ml/8 fl oz/1 cup double (heavy) cream

15 ml/1 tbsp orange flower water

1 Wash and chop the rhubarb. Reserve 25 g/1 oz/2 tbsp of the sugar and put the remainder in a saucepan with the rhubarb, orange zest and juice, and the fresh and ground ginger. Cook over a medium heat for about 15 minutes until the rhubarb has cooked into a thick paste. Make sure you stir it well towards the end so that it does not catch on the bottom of the pan.

2 Add the vanilla essence, then pour into a flat dish to cool. Place in the fridge for about 30–40 minutes to chill.

3 Whip the cream with the reserved sugar and the flower water until stiff. Roughly fold in the rhubarb to give a marbled effect, bringing out the lovely colour of the fruit. Spoon into wine glasses, cover tightly with clingfilm (plastic wrap) and place in the fridge to chill for 2 hours before serving.

Serving suggestions You can serve little langue de chat biscuits (cookies) with the fool, if you like, or my Ginger and Honey Tuille Biscuits (see page 63).

Hints and variations You'll need to prepare the rhubarb well in advance so that it has chance to cool before adding to the cream.

NATURALLY BALANCED Rhubarb is not strictly a fruit (the plant is a member of the same family as buckwheat). It has been used medicinally in Tibet and Mongolia for hundreds of years, but it does contain a dietary oxalate, which is best avoided by anyone prone to forming kidney stones.

Pink grapefruit and lemon granita

A granita is like a sorbet but with a coarse, grainy texture. It makes a perfect end to a summer lunch or you could serve it to refresh the palate after the main course. This recipe takes a little time and attention, but it is well worth the effort as you cannot buy it in shops easily.

MAKES 4–6 PORTIONS

350 ml/12 fl oz/1½ cups water

100 g/4 oz/½ cup unrefined caster (superfine) sugar

200 ml/7 fl oz/scant 1 cup pink grapefruit juice

Grated zest and juice of 1 lemon

1 Pour the water and sugar into a saucepan, bring to a rapid boil, then reduce the heat and simmer until the liquid is reduced to half its original volume.

2 Remove from the heat, add the grapefruit juice and the lemon juice and zest and leave to cool. Pour into a couple of shallow containers and place in the freezer for 25–35 minutes until beginning to form ice crystals. Mash with a fork to break up the ice crystals, then return to the freezer and leave for a further 20 minutes.

3 Repeat the process, mashing and freezing, until you have a hard, dry, crystalline granita. It takes a couple of hours to finish this process, so make sure you have plenty of jobs to do in the house while you attend to it!

4 Serve straight from the freezer, preferably in frosted glasses to keep the granita cold.

Serving suggestions This is delicious on its own, but it also makes a good partner for my Mango and Papaya Cocktail (see page 131).

Hints and variations To frost glasses, place in the freezer until they are ice-cold and have a lovely misty, frozen appearance. Use them immediately as it won't last.

NATURALLY BALANCED Grapefruit are a good source of folic acid, which plays an important part in foetal growth, but they make a useful, refreshing snack whether you are pregnant or not.

Index